Schools that Make the Grade

Schools that Make the Grade

What Successful Schools Do to Improve Student Achievement

by

Martin J.A. Ratcliffe, Ed.D.
Southeastern University
Lakeland, FL

and

Melissa L. Harts, Ed.D.
Hernando County Schools
Brooksville, FL

with invited contributors

·P·A·U·L·H·
BROOKES
PUBLISHING CO. ®

Baltimore • London • Sydney

Paul H. Brookes Publishing Co.
Post Office Box 10624
Baltimore, Maryland 21285-0624
USA

www.brookespublishing.com

"Paul H. Brookes Publishing Co." is a registered trademark
of Paul H. Brookes Publishing Co., Inc.

Typeset by Integrated Publishing Solutions, Grand Rapids, Michigan.
Manufactured in the United States of America by
Victor Graphics, Inc., Baltimore, Maryland.

Some individuals described in this book are composites or real people whose situations are
masked and are based on the authors' experiences. In these instances, names and identifying
details have been changed to protect confidentiality. In certain instances, actual names and
details are used with permission.

Permission to reprint from the following on page 150 is gratefully acknowledged:
Montana Safe Schools Center. (n.d.). *Safe schools assessment and resource bank (SSARB).*
Retrieved September 24, 2010, from http://www.iersum.org/Montana_Safe_Schools_
Center/Safe_Schools_Assessment_SSARB

Cover photo © Image Source Photography/Veer

Library of Congress Cataloging-in-Publication Data

Ratcliffe, Martin J.A.
   Schools that make the grade : what successful schools do to improve student
achievement / by Martin J.A. Ratcliffe ; Melissa L. Harts with invited contributors.
       p.   cm.
   Includes bibliographical references and index.
   ISBN-13: 978-1-59857-090-8 (pbk.)
   ISBN-10: 1-59857-090-0 (pbk.)
   1. School improvement programs—United States.   2. Academic achievement—United
States.   I. Harts, Melissa Lorraine   II. Title.
LB2822.82.R39 2011
371.2′07—dc23   2011017677

British Library Cataloguing in Publication data are available from the British Library.

2015   2014   2013   2012   2011

10   9   8   7   6   5   4   3   2   1

Contents

About the Authors

Martin J.A. Ratcliffe, Ed.D., Assistant Professor, College of Education, Southeastern University, 1000 Longfellow Boulevard, Lakeland, FL 33801

Dr. Ratcliffe is Assistant Professor of Education at Southeastern University in Florida. He earned his certificate in education through the Teachers' Training College in Bulawayo, Rhodesia (now Zimbabwe), and then his bachelor's degree in education through the University of Rhodesia (now Zimbabwe) and his master of arts degree in education and doctor of education degree through Oral Roberts University in Tulsa, Oklahoma. He gives glory to God for enabling him to complete the years of research that laid the foundation for this book. He also expresses a deep heart of gratitude to his beloved Lily of the Valley—his ever-loving and faithful wife Shirley, who has faithfully supported him through the late nights and early mornings; to his two awesome sons, Timothy and Thomas, who sacrificially gave up their dad so that others might benefit; and to their virtuous wives, Carissia and Jerrica, for their love and support. He credits his mother, Mary Ratcliffe, with giving him wings and his father, Brian Ratcliffe, for modeling servant leadership. He thanks his sister, Mary; his late brother, "Kiey"; his brother, Liam; and their families for their support.

Melissa L. Harts, Ed.D., Director of Technology and Information Services, Hernando County Schools, 919 North Broad Street, Brooksville, FL 34601

Dr. Harts is Director of Technology and Information Services for Hernando County Schools in Florida. She is a native of New York, where she attended Fordham University for her undergraduate studies. She later received her first master of science degree from Columbia University Graduate School of Journalism. Following her passion for education and teaching young people, she then enrolled in Columbia University Teachers College, where she received a master's degree in education and a doctorate in instructional technology. She credits her humble accomplishments to her faith and her supportive family, especially her mother, Leonidas Harts, who is the wind beneath her wings; her father, Preston Harts, who is her lighthouse in the storm; her brother Preston Harts, Jr., who is her best friend; and her daughter, Katieri, who is her sole inspiration.

Contributors

Samuel R. Bennett, Ed.D.
Dean
College of Education
Southeastern University
Lakeland, FL

Mary Brezinski, M.Ed.
Director of Faith Formation
   Grades 1–5
St. John Neumann Catholic
   Church
Eagan, MN

Scott Bryan, Ed.D.
Associate Professor
College of Education
Southeastern University
Lakeland, FL

James Dwight Davidson, Ed.D.
Assistant Professor
Graduate School of Education
Oral Roberts University
Tulsa, OK

Glenn S. Gardner, M.Ed.
Teacher
Polk County School Board
Bartow, FL

**Heather Croft Jackson, M.Ed.,
   OTR/L, NBCOT**
National- and State-Certified
   Occupational Therapist

Sonya Jackson, M.Ed.
Assistant Superintendent of
   Schools
Hernando County Schools
Brooksville, FL

Helene Robinson, Ed.D.
ESE Specialist and Assistant
   Education Professor
School of Education
St. John's University, NY

Foreword

... The problems we have discerned in American education can be both understood and corrected if the people of our country, together with those who have public responsibility in the matter, care enough and are courageous enough to do what is required. (Gardner, 1983)

If you "care enough and are courageous enough to do what is required" to improve education, you'll find the work of Martin Ratcliffe and Melissa Harts to be of tremendous value. The authors have assembled for you a summary of research and best practices that produce results, comparative case studies that illustrate similarities and differences behind successful implementation strategies, and practical suggestions that you can pick up and use immediately to build an organizational culture in which learning flourishes for all students.

If you seek ideas and ways in which you can make a difference in the education and lives of future generations, you must read this book.

If you are not convinced of the fact that all children can learn, I ask you to do one thing before setting this book aside. Suspend your disbelief long enough to give the ideas and strategies suggested in this book a try. I can testify, based on two decades of firsthand experience working with hundreds of schools and thousands of educators across this nation, that the body of knowledge commonly referred to as the Effective Schools Research, when implemented, can and will make a significant and positive impact on student performance. The correlates, or characteristics of effective schools as I like to call them, can be replicated in any school. The question is not, "Can we improve education?" The greater question is, "Are we courageous enough to do what is required?"

If you have the courage and desire to do what is required, you can be comforted by the fact that Martin Ratcliffe and Melissa Harts have already prepared a guide to lead you on your journey. One of the keys to success in the journey to improve student achievement is perseverance, finding the courage to continue when hope is replaced by frustration. Let me provide a bit of context.

Education has been an urgent national priority since *A Nation at Risk: The Imperative for Educational Reform* report was released by the National Commission on Excellence in Education in April 1983. The goal to close the achievement gap so that all students—regardless of race, income, or neighborhood—graduate from high school ready to succeed in college and careers was part of this seminal report and has been with us since. We must add to this challenge both state and federal projections of reduced revenues and further cuts in education spending. As education moves closer to concluding three decades of effort to improve education and close the achievement gap, we find ourselves unsuccessful at achieving the goal and our international standing in education to be in decline. We have a system that too often fails our students. Who isn't frustrated?

If we believe a quality education is the key to America's economic growth and prosperity and to our ability to compete in the global economy, we must find strategies that can improve the system.

If we believe a quality education for all students is the path to good jobs, higher earning power, and solutions to the most challenging problems of our time, we do not have the luxury of time—we must act now.

So where do we find hope to keep us going? As I reflect on my experience in working with schools, I find the following truths:

1. Educators, especially teachers, are doing their best to ensure that all students learn.
2. Teachers are willing to improve practice
   - when practical (doable),
   - when manageable (efficient), and
   - when it improves results (effective).
3. School culture determines one's ability to sustain best practice.
4. Systems and structures affect the level of success.
5. Collaboration and collaborative processes can facilitate change.
6. Research-based, data-driven decisions can improve results.
7. Technology can provide many of the tools needed to work smarter and provide teachers, students, and parents with meaningful instructional information—in real time.

If, as educators, we control the variables that effect student success, we can make a difference. Therein lies hope. We, individually and collectively, can make a difference.

As we enter the second decade of the 21st century, there has never been a more pressing need to transform American education and there will never be a better time to act. In keeping with our challenge and priority as a nation, Martin Ratcliffe and Melissa Harts have provided us a common definition of what constitutes an Effective School and offered a plan for action that responds to an urgent national priority and a growing understanding of what educators need to do to ensure all students learn and succeed, keeping our nation competitive in a global economy.

Ben A. Birdsell, M.A.
President
Association for Effective Schools

REFERENCES

Gardner, D.P. (1983, April 26). Letter of transmittal for *A nation at risk: The imperative for educational reform*. Washington, DC: U.S. Government Printing Office.

National Commission on Excellence in Education. (1983). *A nation at risk: The imperative for educational reform*. Washington, DC: U.S. Government Printing Office.

Preface

The No Child Left Behind (NCLB) Act of 2001 (PL 107-110) is powerful federal legislation that is changing the terrain of educational practice in America. Schools are now under enormous pressure to ensure that no child is left behind academically. They are penalized financially if they fail to make adequate yearly progress (AYP) in successive years and can be restructured. The corollary effects have many teachers adjusting their instruction and becoming consumed with student progress. It is this preoccupation with demonstrated learning gains that has gripped attention of schools across America. They are required to demonstrate AYP or else. We wrote *Schools that Make the Grade: What Successful Schools Do to Improve Student Achievement* to bring hope and real-time, research-based solutions to help teachers, principals, and administrators hit the upwardly mobile AYP target year after year. We offer you this book as a token of our gratitude for staying the course and helping all students learn. We invite you to hop on board and journey with us as we share research, vignettes, practical correlate strategies, and ideas that you can use to boost student achievement.

This book was written with passion and compassion for what educators face daily trying to change the world one child at a time. Teachers take work home in overstuffed bags and briefcases; on vacations, they buy motivational trinkets to uplift students or make the class environment more comfortable and conducive to learning; on personal time, they think about ways to help struggling students achieve their goals and how to challenge the average and above average learners to make even greater learning gains. Principals carry the daily burden of making sure that the school community follows the mission of leaving no child behind in any area academically, behaviorally, and socially. They come in before the custodians open the building and leave well after the last teacher closes his or her classroom door. District administrators decipher the mandates from the U.S. Department of Education, monitor progress, administer districtwide trainings, and keep the education ship afloat through the rocky waters of NCLB and Differentiated Accountability.

At each level, educators shoulder the responsibility of NCLB and its federal mandate of AYP. Many strive to do what is best for students, but sometimes it seems that it is not enough. The challenge is great, the frustration is high, but the reward is well worth it. The reward comes when an educator has searched through every available research-based program or strategy to help a student succeed or to turn a school from one in corrective action to one that is leading the pack as an "A" school and has consistently made AYP. The reward comes in the deep laughter from a principal who has presented a teacher with the Teacher of the Year Award. It especially comes from seeing a student smile shyly after finally understanding a concept that he or she has been struggling with academically.

This book was written with the understanding and recognition that educators cannot do it by themselves. They need the support of all community members, including parents, business partners, and politicians. They need to collectively pool their resources, time, and talent to make certain that student achievement is paramount. They can volunteer to help a group of elementary school students learn to read, take a day from their daily routines to attend a high school presentation, or share the school data with parents and encourage them to help their child at home. There are so many other examples of collaborative solutions that can help propel students forward and make a difference in their lives.

Schools that Make the Grade offers research-based strategies and basic instructional best practices through the lens of effective school correlates. In this book, we look at what schools are doing and have done effectively in the areas of 1) Positive Home–School Relations, 2) Opportunity to Learn and Student Time on Task, 3) Climate of High Expectations, 4) Clear and Focused Mission, 5) Frequent Monitoring of Student Progress, 6) Instructional Leadership, and 7) Safe and Orderly Environment. By examining these correlates, we offer suggestions to the three-tiered level of educational leadership needed to support learning gains in schools: the district/state level, the principal/school level, and the teacher/classroom level. It is our sincere intention that this book will show educators how to boost student achievement and help schools make the grade by effectively implementing each of the seven correlates.

We have pooled our experience in education to interview and question colleagues on the front lines of education. This book contains suggestions and experiences from superintendents, principals, teachers, and parents. The insight gleaned from their stories coupled with the research creates a reference guide for educators to use as a tool in the NCLB arena. However, the most important point—which we, the authors, hope does not get lost in the interviews, case studies, and researched strategies—is the intention to offer help to our fellow colleagues whom we have not met and may never know other than the time we share throughout the course of this book.

We hope that as you take this journey with us, you realize that we are trying to provide beacons of light as we go through this era of accountability together. We are not on the mountaintop preaching to the masses; we are part of the team marching in the direction toward effective and consistent school achievement, where every student learns regardless of his or her background or academic ability. We march to the beat of the correlates hoping that others will follow, and we share with you some of the experiences that we and others have had along the way.

We have both spent years in the classroom and have worked as administrators. Melissa Harts started as a secondary school teacher, became an assistant principal for a public school for kindergarten through Grade 8, and then became a district-level administrator. She has taught in higher education as well. Martin Ratcliffe began as a public school elementary teacher and then a principal in Zimbabwe. He later came to the United States and was an elementary school teacher, an elementary and middle school principal, and then a grade administrator in private school education for preschool through Grade 12 before returning to public school teaching. He is currently an assistant education professor at a university in Florida. This book is the combined result of those experiences, which we now humbly offer you. We have felt your frustration at all levels. We have hovered over the data and pondered how to move students and demonstrate learning gains. We have researched and implemented strategies in our classrooms, in our schools, and at the district level to promote student achievement and help schools make the grade.

From the researcher's perspective, the bipartisan NCLB legislation passed during the Bush administration was akin to a majestic cumulonimbus thundercloud held gently by the warm and far-reaching fingers of the sun's rays. But down on the ground, from a school- and district-level perspective, the weather did not always seem as fair. In fact, there were unannounced cloudbursts of more paperwork, more accountability, and more tightening of the reins.

Helping schools improve student achievement is the passion of both authors, who have approached it from different perspectives. Martin Ratcliffe's (2006) research shows that the seven correlates discussed in this book are present in effective schools regardless of the school's socioeconomic status. Melissa Harts's interviews with professionals on the front lines brings a much-needed "reality approach" to the practical implementation of correlate strategies that work at the grass-roots level. We have invited highly effective professionals—including Samuel Bennett, Mary Brezinski, Glenn Gardner, Helene Robinson, Sonya Jackson, Scott Bryan, James Dwight Davidson, and Heather Jackson—to share supportive research and anecdotal contributions to further enrich the book. We also invited Janet Deck and Amy Bratten to share some key strategies for maximizing learning opportunities and enhancing academic achievement.

Steering your educational ship by the correlate beacons outlined in this book can help you navigate the sometimes turbulent waters of change and uncertainty and help you avoid shipwreck. You must stay focused on what really matters academically and operationalize the correlates to sail your educational ship into the quiet harbors of academic success by boosting student achievement across the board so that schools make the grade. This book shows you how to do that.

ORGANIZATION OF THE BOOK

The book is arranged in 10 chapters. Chapter 1 introduces two almost identical case study schools. One consistently made an "A" grade and AYP, whereas the other made an "A" grade fairly consistently but failed to make AYP. We delve into case study comparison to compare and contrast strategies used by both schools and explore lessons to be learned. The remainder of Chapter 1 discusses NCLB, AYP, Differentiated Accountability, and the future of NCLB as laid out in the Obama administration's Blueprint for Reform: The Reauthorization of the Elementary and Secondary Education Act proposal (U.S. Department of Education, 2010). It concludes by acknowledging the AYP/student achievement crisis while briefly introducing the solution to the crisis—which is the subject of this book.

Chapter 2 introduces the reader to the seven correlates and presents compelling research to show that effective schools have a strong presence of the correlates. It presents studies that link the correlates to student achievement, including Martin Ratcliffe's (2006) study that demonstrates a significant relationship between the correlates and AYP. Key findings and implications of this study are discussed. The chapter closes by introducing the need for the operationalization, or putting into practice strategies to boost the presence of the correlates and therefore student learning and achievement scores.

Chapters 3–9 introduce the seven correlates: Positive Home–School Relations, Opportunity to Learn and Student Time on Task, Climate of High Expectations, Clear Vision and Mission, Frequent Monitoring of Student Progress, Instructional Leadership, and Safe and Orderly Environment. Chapters 3–9 focus on these correlates by presenting case studies, vignettes, perspectives, frontline quotes, and supportive research. Correlate strategies for improving student achievement are distilled from these streams of knowledge and experience and reported in terms of what highly effective superintendents and district administrators do, what highly effective principals and school administrators do, and what highly effective teachers do. Each chapter concludes with chapter reflection questions for individual or group study.

Finally, Chapter 10 briefly revisits the AYP/student achievement crisis, reviews the antidote (correlate solutions), conducts case study reflections, highlights key lessons to be learned from the book, appeals to educators to stop playing what might be called the "AYP game," and exhorts educators to believe in themselves and their calling so they can positively influence the lives of students by improving student achievement. We end by challenging educators to focus on the operationalization of the research-supported bedrock correlates of effective schools—in doing so, they should reap the rewards of increasing student achievement and making AYP.

CLOSING THOUGHTS

We envision this book as a reference guide for pre- or in-service teachers and educators and instructional leaders who are struggling with daily administrative challenges, the weight of the NCLB federal mandate, and the scrutiny of data-driven accountability. We hope that the wealth of practical correlate solutions and ideas embedded in the book will serve as a beacon of light in an overwhelmingly clouded educational arena that is shrouded with AYP requirements and no definitive way to meet them. It is our desire that this book will offer educators a clear response—a way to navigate NCLB, to address accountability, and to emerge stronger, wiser, and with an arsenal of proven correlate strategies to buttress best practices, affect student learning, and improve student achievement scores so that schools make the grade.

REFERENCES

No Child Left Behind Act of 2001, PL 107-110, 115 Stat. 1425, 20 U.S.C. §§ 6301 et seq.

Ratcliffe, M.J.A. (2006). *A study of the relationship between the correlates of effective schools and aggregate adequate yearly progress.* Retrieved February 23, 2011, from gradworks.umi.com/32/56/3256628.html

U.S. Department of Education. (2010). *A blueprint for reform: The reauthorization of the Elementary and Secondary Education Act.* Retrieved July 28, 2010, from http://www2.ed.gov/policy/elsec/leg/blueprint/blueprint.pdf

Acknowledgements

Sincere acknowledgements are made to the following for their contribution to this book:

- Case study contributors Dave Dannemiller, M.Ed., and Marcia Austin, Ed.D.
- Chapter contributors Samuel Bennett, Ed.D.; Mary Brezinski, M.Ed.; Glenn Gardner, M.Ed.; Helene Robinson, Ed.D; Sonya Jackson, M.Ed.; Scott Bryan, Ed.D.; James Dwight Davidson, Ed.D.; and Heather Jackson, M.Ed.
- Chapter 4 table contributors Janet Deck, Ed.D., and Amy Bratten, M.A. TESOL
- Those who contributed vignettes and perspectives and those who completed surveys and interviews
- Brookes Publishing's editors, for their timely and specific feedback that enabled us to write with precision

We also express sincere appreciation to our families, friends, students, and colleagues who have supported us in this exciting venture, and we give special thanks to Our Lord, Jesus Christ—the Master Teacher—for His grace to write this book.

*This book is dedicated to helping frontline educators
at all levels become highly effective and improve student learning.*

The Adequate Yearly Progress/Student Achievement Crisis

Today's [National Assessment of Educational Progress] results once again show that the achievement of American students isn't growing fast enough. . . . Students aren't making the progress necessary to compete in the global economy. . . . Our students aren't on a path to graduate high school ready to succeed in college and the workplace.

—U.S. Secretary of Education Arne Duncan
(U.S. Department of Education, 2010b, p. 1).

Our journey begins gently with a preview of two case study schools, which will be revisited in each of Chapters 3–9 to illustrate how effective schools look in practice. We then delve into the intricacies of the No Child Left Behind Act of 2001 (NCLB; PL 107-110) and its accompanying high-stakes adequate yearly progress (AYP) accountability. We take a brief look at Differentiated Accountability being piloted in a number of states, and then peek into the future by examining the Obama administration's stance on education, including the Race to the Top competition and the Blueprint for Reform: The Reauthorization of the Elementary and Secondary Education Act proposal. We close this introductory chapter by offering hope for the student achievement crisis and pointing the reader to the solution to the crisis—which is the topic in Chapter 2 and the subject of this book.

CASE STUDY
SCHOOL 1

Hidden at the end of a long road in Florida, an elementary school sits as an inconspicuous neighbor to a middle school. The branches from the drooping cypress trees on each side of the road create an open archway, welcoming visitors to the winding road leading to the visitors' parking area. Judging by looks alone, one would assume the plain, U-shaped, one-story building trimmed in navy blue with a placard sign out front is just a typical elementary school. Through the iron fence surrounding it, you can glimpse a well-kept playground on the right, the cafeteria windows straight ahead, and the inviting administration building directly to the left.

Nothing about the exterior of this place of learning or the busyness of the teachers passing down the corridors of the open campus suggests that this school, Pine Grove Elementary, is the only Title I school in its district that has made AYP consecutively for 2 years and has maintained a state of Florida school grade of "A" consecutively for 6 years. The 2 AYP years of reference are 2006–2007 and 2007–2008. In the 2008–2009 school year, Pine Grove Elementary maintained an "A" grade; however, the school did not make AYP. Based on the results of the statewide standardized test for that year, the Florida Comprehensive Assessment Test (FCAT), Pine Grove Elementary tested 577 students, which was 100% of its student population in third through fifth grades (Florida Department of Education, 2010). That number accounts for 61% of its students receiving free and reduced lunch. To qualify for Title I, a district must have at least a 35% poverty rate. However, districts can set their own percentages for their schools as long as they meet the minimum required percentage by ranking their schools according to the geographic location and poverty levels (U.S. Department of Education, 2003). From 2008 to 2009, the Title I criteria for the Hernando County School District was 50% free and reduced lunch. (Fifty percent of a school's population must receive free and reduced lunch.) In 2008–2009 FCAT testing, 81% of the students met the standards in reading, 74% met the standards for math, and 46% met the standards in science. In addition, 82% of the fourth graders met the standards in writing (Florida Department of Education, 2010).

For a Title I school to maintain an "A" grade for 6 years in a row and to achieve AYP for 2 consecutive years is an impressive track record, given that it has had several hundreds of students and dozens of teachers pass through its doors. It has gone through renovations, adding portable classrooms to address its student growth, and has had three principals in the history of the 23-year-old school. One of the principals, Dave Dannemiller, held the job for 9 years. He was the school's instructional leader at the time it made AYP for 2 years consecutively. Now a middle school principal, Dannemiller reflected on what contributed to the Pine Grove's maintaining an "A" grade and making AYP under his leadership. He emphasized that the students' success rested on the shoulders of the teachers and the strategies that they employed in their classrooms coupled with the level of parental support. He said, "When parents buy in, there's a can-do attitude that is built in. [Principals also have to] create a mind-set of no excuses with teachers and students, especially when it comes to analyzing the data and actually doing something with it. [Principals must ask] now that we have that information, what are we going to do to change—to improve?"

In addition, he said, he created a culture where teachers discussed, monitored, shaped, and reflected on student learning. "It takes a while to build that climate where people are accepting the fact that they have to look at the data, be honest with the data, and look at the fact that they are in fidelity with implementing the strategies for it. You have to have a lot of buy in and it takes a lot of giving from both the teachers and the leadership to get it," Dannemiller said. Similar to many principals across the country who have had to build a climate of learning in their schools, Dannemiller stressed that he focused on a plethora of student data and applauded teachers who were adopting innovative and effective instructional practices in response to it. These teachers then became role models for their peers and were expected to mentor their colleagues on their respective teams.

It seems that this teacher mentoring helped to strengthen the bonds in the school, which were interwoven with effective practices, sound instructional methodology, data-driven accountability, and constant and consistent progress monitoring. Dannemiller said that this was not an easy feat and that it took at least 3 years for him to truly get the school in alignment with these crucial core ingredients that increase student achievement and affect AYP scores. "Achieving AYP is an art and a science. It's an art because you have to be creative in collaboration and instruction. It is scientific because you must analyze the data and have measureable outcomes as you implement strategies for improvement," he said.

STRATEGIES FOR INCREASING STUDENT ACHIEVEMENT

Although the principal and staff at Pine Grove worked collaboratively and focused on the crucial core ingredients for making and sustaining AYP for 2 consecutive years, the principal aptly pointed out that there is no formulaic structure for guaranteed success. Research-based strategies can be combined to transform an ineffective school into an effective one, but there is no easy one-size-fits-all formula. Schools must make AYP despite the daily challenges, including a transient population, overcrowding, lack of sufficient resources, high teacher turnover, and a decrease in district-level and school-based administrative staff. Schools today must plow through the consortium of challenges and still show an increase in student achievement, although the variables change year to year.

These challenges sometimes overtake a school's best efforts to show annual growth in student learning gains, resulting in a "good" school with an "A" grade not making AYP.

CASE STUDY
SCHOOL 2

An example of a grade "A" school not making AYP is found in a school less than 10 miles from Pine Grove. Just across the interstate, on the opposite side of town, another neighborhood school sits in the center of a quiet community. It has the same shape and design as Pine Grove, with manicured lawns and a welcoming layout. An array of flowers are in bloom, and in the courtyard is a student-made pond. Along the walkway, speakers disguised as stones play soft music. To the far right in the back, a new "concreteable" building (i.e., a portable building made from concrete) replaces the old portable classrooms (trailers) that provided space for the once-overcrowded school.

However, no matter how hard you look, there is no glaring sign that lets you know that John D. Floyd, a non-Title I school, was an "A" school 4 years in a row—a noteworthy accomplishment given that it also added a middle school during that time. Unlike its sister school, Pine Grove, the 25-year-old John D. Floyd (also known as John D. Floyd K-8 Environmental Science School because of its middle school addition) did not make AYP any of those years. It was not for lack of trying. One of the authors of this book, Melissa Harts, a former assistant principal there, worked with the principal in stressing the crucial core ingredients, which included effective practices, sound instructional methodology, data-driven accountability, and constant and consistent progress monitoring.

According to the data from the Florida Department of Education (2010) for the 2008–2009 school year, John D. Floyd maintained an "A" grade; however, as noted previously, the school again did not make AYP. Based on the FCAT results for that year, John D. Floyd tested 632 students, which was 100% of its student population in third through eighth grades. That number accounts for 51% of its students receiving free and reduced lunch (it was the first year John D. Floyd had more than 50% of its students qualify for free and reduced lunch). Despite these percentages, John D. Floyd did not qualify for Title I funds because the Title I funds were allocated to the schools with the highest need. Similar to Pine Grove's scores for that school year, 81% of the tested students met the standards in FCAT reading scores. At John D. Floyd, 73% of tested students met the standards for math (which is 1% lower than the same scores for Pine Grove) and 58% met the standards in science. Of the fourth and eighth graders, 90% met the standards in writing (Florida Department Of Education, 2010). Table 1.1 summarizes the data from the two schools.

The principal at the time, Dr. Marcia Austin, who later became a curriculum supervisor for the district, reflected on the core ingredients to

Table 1.1. Summary of data from the two case study schools

2008–2009 school year	Pine Grove	John D. Floyd
Title I school?	Yes	No
Percentage of students receiving free and reduced lunch	61	51
Consecutive years making adequate yearly progress (AYP)	2	0
Consecutive years making "A" grade	6	4
Number tested	577	632
Percentage of students tested	100	100
Percentage of students meeting reading standards	81	81
Percentage of students meeting math standards	74	73
Percentage of students meeting writing standards	82	90
Percentage of students meeting science standards	46	58

making AYP in an interview. She said, "We focused on our purpose, became consistent in what we did from grade to grade, classroom to classroom, and subject to subject. We collaborated and made sure we supported ongoing progress monitoring." Specifically, she encouraged teachers to collaborate and make connections throughout the inter- and intra-grade level. Similar to the strategies used at Pine Grove, John D. Floyd also used teacher mentors, insisted on common planning, and encouraged introspection and reflection on instructional strategies that promoted student learning gains.

But what was the difference? Although both schools maintained an "A" grade, Pine Grove was able to maintain AYP for 2 consecutive years, whereas John D. Floyd could not achieve AYP. Austin explained, "The school has a high mobility rate, a number of subgroups, and a high population of students with exceptionalities. Limited resources made it difficult to consistently and effectively target every identified subgroup." She said that high teacher turnover and student population growth initially made it challenging when trying to achieve AYP and maintain an "A" grade. She said that as the years passed, these challenges were counterbalanced with the implementation of structures, routines, and support systems that offset the turnover and student growth.

CASE STUDY ANALYSIS

Questions remain as to what strategies, structures, and routines both schools put in place. Chapters 3–9 explore these questions in detail and compare what worked at both schools and what did not. A comparative analysis of each school's culture, leadership style, teaching methodology, and home–school relationships will pave the way for a deeper understanding of the successful practices and strategies implemented that helped both schools, though different, maintain an "A" grade. The chapters also look at the distinction between them that resulted in one school achieving and maintaining AYP and at possible reasons why the other did not. In addition, each chapter provides perspectives from frontline educators—superintendents, principals, and teachers—and digs into the research before revealing clear correlate strategies that educators can and, in fact, *must* use to boost student learning and AYP scores. Correlates are constructs or characteristics of effective schools identified in multiple studies as being "co-related" to exceptional student achievement (Stringfield, 2004). To prepare for these explorations, the next section provides more background on NCLB.

NO CHILD LEFT BEHIND ACT OF 2001

The 1965 Elementary and Secondary Education Act (ESEA; PL 89-10) came about following a few federal initiatives in the education system from the 1950s—most significantly the Supreme Court ruling *Brown v. Board of Education* (1954) to eliminate segregated schools and the 1958 National Defense Education Act (PL 85-864) that provided funding for students in higher education and for school construction. The National Defense Education Act was prompted by the Soviet launch of the satellite Sputnik— almost overnight, a call arose for increased academic standards, a greater focus on mathematics and science, and the inclusion of foreign language education in schools (Ravitch, 2000). The ESEA further increased the federal government's role in public education by providing funds to help low-income students, and it resulted in the initiation of educational programs such as Title I, Head Start, and bilingual education (Sass, 2005). The ESEA has been reauthorized several times, and most recently its reauthorization was named the No Child Left Behind Act of 2001. This reauthorization of the act focuses on holding schools accountable for student achievement levels and providing penalties for schools that do not make AYP toward full student proficiency. As of 2010, nearly a decade following NCLB, another reauthorization of the legislation (once more called ESEA) is pending that will once again redefine the educational landscape.

What Exactly Is No Child Left Behind?

In a nutshell, NCLB is "a landmark in education reform designed to improve student achievement and close achievement gaps" (U.S. Department of Education, 2004, p. 1). NCLB was founded on several guiding principles. Figure 1.1 summarizes key components of NCLB.

What Exactly Is NCLB?

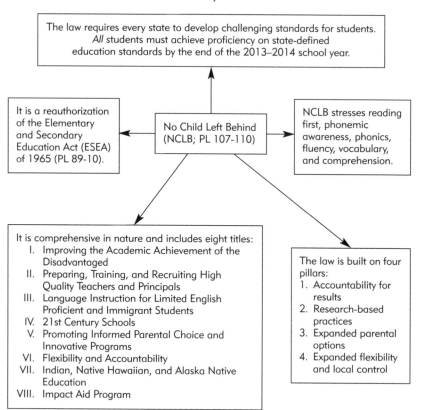

The law requires every state to develop challenging standards for students. *All* students must achieve proficiency on state-defined education standards by the end of the 2013–2014 school year.

It is a reauthorization of the Elementary and Secondary Education Act (ESEA) of 1965 (PL 89-10).

No Child Left Behind (NCLB; PL 107-110)

NCLB stresses reading first, phonemic awareness, phonics, fluency, vocabulary, and comprehension.

It is comprehensive in nature and includes eight titles:
  I. Improving the Academic Achievement of the Disadvantaged
  II. Preparing, Training, and Recruiting High Quality Teachers and Principals
  III. Language Instruction for Limited English Proficient and Immigrant Students
  IV. 21st Century Schools
  V. Promoting Informed Parental Choice and Innovative Programs
  VI. Flexibility and Accountability
  VII. Indian, Native Hawaiian, and Alaska Native Education
  VIII. Impact Aid Program

The law is built on four pillars:
  1. Accountability for results
  2. Research-based practices
  3. Expanded parental options
  4. Expanded flexibility and local control

Figure 1.1. Key components of the No Child Left Behind Act of 2001 (PL 107-110).

Perspective

Shortly after my transition back to the classroom from private school administration, I (Martin Ratcliffe) had a growing sense of tectonic changes deep inside public education. The advent of the NCLB legislation and the arrival of a new school principal sparked a series of painful systemic alignments that ushered teachers into a keen awareness of data-driven teaching, with its accompanying accountability grip. Gone were the days of just being a good teacher. Teachers were now held accountable for student learning gains regardless of the student's background. Students in different subgroups had to make AYP, and achievement gaps between subgroups had to decrease.

It was evident that landmark legislation was beginning to take effect and that the iron jaws of accountability for results were sinking their teeth into every facet of education. Internally, from a teacher's perspective, I could sense

a buildup of pressure for the accountability of student learning. This trans-
lated into more paperwork, which I termed "administrivia"—all the extra
things that needed to be done that did not necessarily correlate directly with
improvements in student learning but were necessary from an accountability
standpoint. For example, progress monitoring in reading required frequent
documentation of students' reading rates, initially by hand and later on
through a computer tracking system. This sounds like a great idea in theory
(and it is), but in reality it required significant amounts of classroom teaching
time. In addition, school fundraisers (which teachers promoted and for which
they kept track of the money) and a plethora of nonacademic activities that
required teachers to keep track of paperwork still remained.

In my mind, the school needed to rethink its priorities and align its prac-
tices with the new mission of NCLB. The elimination of some nonacademic
activities would have eased the pressure and allowed some room for the in-
creased accountability measures. Regardless, more was expected of teach-
ers and very little, if anything, was removed from the growing mountain of
teacher responsibilities. It seemed that AYP could also mean "All Your Pupils"
(No Child Left Behind), "All Your Passion" (working harder), "All Your Poten-
tial" (working smarter), "All Your Patience" (increased demands on the
teacher), "All Your Pay" (more teacher resources), "All Your Pressure" (in-
creased stress levels), or "All Your Parents" (building positive home–school
relationships).

Adequate Yearly Progress

John Hughes (formerly from the Florida Department of Education's Office of Evaluation and Reporting and currently the overseer of the institutional research and effectiveness unit within the Division of Florida Colleges) noted that AYP is a federal designation based upon meeting specific criteria set forth by states (personal communication, July 12, 2005). Duran (2005) noted that it is intended to measure "continuous and substantial yearly improvement toward achieving proficiency and advanced performance levels" (p. 11).

Each state must establish its own criteria for meeting AYP within the parameters of NCLB and hold schools and districts within the state accountable for meeting AYP. Each state is required to establish a single statewide accountability system that effectively measures student academic achievement in the following delineated subgroups: low-income students, students from major racial and ethnic groups, students with disabilities, and students with limited English proficiency. At least 95% of students in each group must be tested in order for the school to make AYP. States establish their AYP criteria targeting the minimum percentage of students who must realize proficiency in reading and language arts, mathematics, and science. These annual AYP targets increase at least once every 3 years until 2013–2014, when all students should achieve proficiency (U.S. Department of Education, 2004).

What Happens When a Federally Funded
School Does Not Make Adequate Yearly Progress?

There are no sanctions for schools that fail to make AYP the first year.

The second year entails identification of schools and districts in need of improvement. Schools receiving Title I funds are reviewed annually to ensure that they are making AYP. Schools and districts that fail to make AYP for 2 consecutive years are identified as in need of improvement (U.S. Department of Education, 2002). Identified schools must develop a 2-year plan to remedy the anomalies. They must provide students with the option of transferring to a successful public or charter school in the district, with transportation provided. These schools must spend at least 10% of their Title I Part A funds on professional development programs for teachers and principals that directly address the academic achievement problems that caused the school not to make AYP (U.S. Department of Education, n.d.-c).

The third year involves supplemental educational services. In addition to second-year sanctions, schools failing to make AYP for 3 consecutive years must inform parents of students from low-income families of their eligibility to receive Title I funds for supplemental services, such as tutoring or remedial classes. Parents are permitted to select services from approved public or private school providers, including faith-based organizations (U.S. Department of Education, 2002).

The fourth year is marked by corrective action. In the fourth consecutive year of a federally funded (Title 1) school failing to make AYP, a school district must take corrective action aimed at bringing about meaningful school change. In addition to second- and third-year sanctions, school districts must select one of the following options: replace school staff, fully implement a new curriculum (with appropriate professional development), decrease management authority at the school level, appoint an outside expert to advise the school, extend the school day or year, or reorganize the school internally (U.S. Department of Education, 2002).

According to the U.S. Department of Education,

> Similarly, if a school district fails to make adequate yearly progress for four years, the state must take corrective actions that must include at least one of the following: deferring programmatic funds or reducing administrative funds; implementing a new curriculum (with professional development); replacing personnel; establishing alternative governance arrangements ; appointing a receiver or trustee to administer the district in place of the superintendents and school board ; or abolishing or restructuring the school district. The state may also authorize students to transfer to higher-performing public schools operated by another school district (with transportation). States must provide information to parents and the public of any corrective action the state takes with school districts. (2002, p. 7)

The fifth year is marked for restructuring. Failure to make AYP for the fifth consecutive year results in a school district initiating a fundamental restructuring of the school. According to the U.S. Department of Education (2004), such restructuring may include "reopening the school as a charter school, replacing all or most of the staff, or turning over school operations either to the state or a private company with a demonstrated record of effectiveness" (p. 7).

According to the U.S. Department of Education (2004), at all levels of identification, technical assistance must be implemented: "State assistance must include establishing school support teams; designating and using distinguished teachers and principals; providing assistance through institutions of higher education . . . or private providers of scientifically based technical assistance" (p. 7).

Differentiated Accountability

The term *Differentiated Accountability* is an initiative by the federal government to make it easier for schools to comply with the rigorous NCLB accountability. States apply for permission to implement it. The Differentiated Accountability Model, also known as the Differentiated Accountability Matrix, makes it very clear that non-Title I schools in corrective action will receive the same sanctions as Title I schools, including the state department of education taking over the school and the principal being removed because a school has failed to meet AYP for 2 consecutive years. Although for years legislation has spelled out corrective action and consequences for schools not making AYP, the Differentiated Accountability Model holds districts accountable for the AYP scores of non-Title I schools as well. It delineates what districts must do in order to meet the NCLB mandates. For example, if a school is showing poor gains in math and science scores, the district must provide a resource coach for those schools. There also must be a plan of action that includes progress monitoring, teacher evaluation walk-throughs, and documentation. The U.S. Department of Education makes it clear that "states' differentiated accountability models must maintain the current measurement of adequate yearly progress (AYP) under section 1111 of NCLB" (2008, p. 1).

According to Bob Schaeffer, Public Education Director of FairTest: National Center for Fair & Open Testing,

> Differentiated accountability [was designed] to reduce the growing political pressure calling for a comprehensive overhaul of the federal No Child Left Behind (NCLB) law. Implemented as a pilot program in the final year of George W. Bush's presidency, the initiative by U.S. Department of Education Secretary Margaret Spellings allows selected states some flexibility in implementing NCLB's schedule of sanctions for schools and districts which do not attain Adequate Yearly Progress

(AYP). [The] program simply allows minor options within NCLB's rigid accountability model. Thus, Differentiated Accountability may temporarily tone down criticism of NCLB by political leaders in the 17 states where it is in effect. (personal communication, July 29, 2009)

OBAMA ADMINISTRATION'S STANCE ON EDUCATION

According to the Blueprint for Reform (U.S. Department of Education, 2010a), President Obama appears to consider education a national priority and endorses education reform that will provide a world-class education for every child. He has proposed what has become known as the "Five Pillars" of the American reformation agenda for the educational system with an emphasis on the reauthorization of NCLB. The five pillars are 1) investing in early childhood initiatives; 2) encouraging better standards and assessments; 3) recruiting, preparing, and rewarding outstanding teachers; 4) promoting innovation and excellence in America's schools; and 5) providing every American with a higher quality education (The White House Blog, 2009).

Secretary of Education Arne Duncan, a former superintendent of Chicago schools, strongly supports the education vision of the Obama administration:

> Taken together—the Barack effect—the leadership on the Hill—the proven strategies—and the money in the stimulus package—represent what I call—the perfect storm for reform—a historic alignment of interests and events that could lift American education to an entirely new level. (U.S. Department of Education, 2009b)

Duncan believes that education is the single most important issue in America today, as it affects America's ability to compete globally. He said,

> I don't need to tell you that America has lost its global leadership in education. K–12 achievement levels leave millions of young people unprepared for work or for college. This is a national crisis that is rapidly creating an entire class of Americans who are unable to share in the benefits of a modern, progressive and productive society. There simply are no good jobs for people without an education. Given the state of our economy, the pace of technological change, and the scope of our collective challenges—no other issue is more pressing. (U.S. Department of Education, 2009b)

On February 17, 2009, President Obama signed the American Recovery and Reinvestment Act (ARRA) of 2009 (PL 111-5) into law. The act is the federal government's response to the economic crisis and a strategic attempt to jumpstart the economy. It provides billions of stimulus dollars for education and training and is designed to help schools raise academic achievement under NCLB (U.S. Department of Education, 2009a). In addition, the Race to the Top state competition is an unprecedented federal investment in education reform that set aside $4.35 billion for education reform: $4 billion for statewide reform grants and $350 million for states working to improve their assessments. The Race to the Top competition rewards states that lead the way in "comprehensive, coherent, statewide education reform" (U.S. Department of Education, 2010c).

Blueprint for Reform

President Barack Obama's Blueprint for Reform sets out a clear vision and proposal for the reauthorization of the ESEA. According to the Blueprint for Reform, President Obama's vision is that "every child in America deserves a world-class education" (U.S. Department of Education, 2010a, p. 1).

The Blueprint for Reform builds around four significant reform areas that were made in response to the ARRA of 2009, namely,

> (1) Improving teacher and principal effectiveness to ensure that every classroom has a great teacher and every school has a great leader; (2) Providing information to families to help them evaluate and improve their children's schools, and to educators to help them improve their students' learning; (3) Implementing college- and career-ready standards and developing improved assessments aligned with those standards; and (4) Improving student learning and achievement in America's lowest-performing schools by providing intensive support and effective interventions. (U.S. Department of Education, 2010a, p. 1)

In addition to rectifying the perceived NCLB anomalies and paving the way for a reauthorized ESEA, the blueprint for a re-envisioned federal role in education has identified five priorities that build on the above framework: 1) College and Career Readiness; 2) Great Teachers and Leaders in Every School; 3) Equity and Opportunity for All Students; 4) Raise the Bar and Reward Excellence; and 5) Promote Innovation and Continuous Improvement. Table 1.2 compares NCLB and the proposed reauthorization of ESEA in the Blueprint for Reform.

College and Career Readiness   The U.S. Department of Education recognizes the efforts by NCLB to raise academic standards. However, it realizes that further improvement is needed to prepare students for college and careers. Consequently, the U.S. Department of Education (2010a) intends to raise standards for all students, offer better assessments, and provide a complete education to students: "We will set a clear goal: Every student should graduate from high school ready for college and a career, regardless of their income, race, ethnic or language background, or disability status" (p. 4). The U.S. Department of Education supports "a new generation of assessments that are aligned with college- and career-ready standards, to better determine whether students have acquired the skills they need for success" (U.S. Department of Education, 2010a, p. 4). According to the Blueprint for Reform, "Students need a well-rounded education to contribute

Table 1.2 NCLB and pending ESEA reauthorization comparison

	No Child Left Behind (NCLB; PL 107-110)	Elementary and Secondary Education Act (ESEA of 1965 [PL 89-10], pending reauthorization)
Vision	No Child Left Behind	Every child deserves a world-class education
Foundational pillars/reform areas	1. Accountability for Results	"(1) Improving teacher and principal effectiveness . . .
	2. Research-Based Practices	(2) Providing information to families . . . and . . . educators to . . . improve . . . students' learning;
	3. Expanded Parental Options	(3) Implementing college- and career-ready standards and developing improved assessments . . .
	4. Expanded Flexibility and Control	(4) Improving student learning and achievement in America's lowest-performing schools. . . ." (U.S. Department of Education, 2010a, p. 3)
School/teacher	Schools must make adequate yearly progress (AYP).	Teacher assessment will be based in significant part on "student growth and also include other measures, such as classroom observations of practice" (U.S. Department of Education, 2010a, p. 14).
What subjects are assessed?	Math, reading, writing, science	Complete education (assessment is still to be determined, but may include literacy, mathematics, science, technology, history, civics, foreign languages, the arts, financial literacy, and other subjects).
Teacher qualifications	"A highly qualified teacher must have: • A bachelor's degree. • Full state certification, as defined by the state. • Demonstrated competency, as defined by the state, in each core academic subject he or she teaches" (U.S. Department of Education, 2004, p. 10)	"Statewide definitions of 'effective teacher,' 'effective principal,' 'highly effective teacher,' and 'highly effective principal' developed in collaboration with teachers, principals, and other stakeholders" (U.S. Department of Education, 2010a, p. 14)

as citizens in our democracy and to thrive in a global economy—from literacy to mathematics, science, and technology to history, civics, foreign languages, the arts, financial literacy, and other subjects" (U.S. Department of Education, 2010a, p. 5). The U.S. Department of Education will support efforts for a more complete education "through improved professional development and evidence-based instructional models and supports" (U.S. Department of Education, 2010a, p. 5).

Great Teachers and Leaders in Every School   Under NCLB, "A highly qualified teacher must have: a bachelor's degree . . . full state certification, as defined by the state, and . . . demonstrated competency, as defined by the state, in each core academic subject he or she teaches" (U.S. Department of Education, 2004, p. 10). The proposed Blueprint for Reform uses the terms *effective* and *highly effective* in reference to teachers and principals. The Blueprint for Reform calls for states and districts to "identify effective and highly effective teachers and principals on the basis of student growth and other factors" (U.S. Department of Education, 2010a, p. 4). The Blueprint for Reform puts a renewed emphasis on placing effective teachers and principals in high-need schools. It also recognizes the need to more effectively prepare, place, and support beginning teachers and principals in high-need schools.

Equity and Opportunity for All Students   According to the Blueprint for Reform, "All students will be included in an accountability system that builds on college- and career-ready standards, rewards progress and success, and requires rigorous interventions in the lowest-performing schools" (U.S. Department of Education, 2010a, p. 6). This appears to be similar to NCLB, but the emphasis is on college and career readiness. The Blueprint for Reform stresses the need for meeting the diverse needs of all learners regardless of their educational status or societal position. These learners include students from "English learners and students with disabilities, to Native American students, homeless students, migrant students, rural students, and neglected or delinquent students" (U.S. Department of Education, 2010a, p. 6). The ESEA proposal emphasizes greater equity for all and promises to level the playing field by "moving toward comparability in resources between high- and low-poverty schools" (U.S. Department of Education, 2010a, p. 6).

Raise the Bar and Reward Excellence   The Blueprint for Reform proposes three keys to raising the academic bar and rewarding excellence. First, the U.S. Department of Education will "continue the Race to the Top's incentives for systemic reforms at the state level and expand the program to school districts that are willing to take on bold, comprehensive reforms" (U.S. Department of Education, 2010a, p. 7). Second, the Blueprint for Reform proposes supporting effective school choice by supporting "the expansion of high-performing public charter schools and other autonomous public schools, and support[ing] local communities as they expand public school choice options for students within and across school districts" (U.S. Department of Education, 2010a, p. 7). Third, the Blueprint for Reform promotes a culture of college readiness and success: "Access to a challenging high school curriculum has a greater impact on whether a student will earn a 4-year college degree than his or her high school test scores, class rank, or grades" (U.S. Department of Education, 2010a, p. 7).

Promote Innovation and Continuous Improvement Fostering innovation and accelerating success is one goal in promoting innovation and continuous improvement. The Investing in Innovation Fund will assist local and nonprofit leaders in their quest to "develop and scale up programs that have demonstrated success, and discover the next generation of innovative solutions" (U.S. Department of Education, 2010a, p. 7). Another goal is supporting, recognizing, and rewarding local innovation. The idea is for less red tape and the creation of "fewer, larger, more flexible funding streams around areas integral to student success, giving states and districts flexibility to focus on local needs" (U.S. Department of Education, 2010a, p. 7). A third goal is supporting student success. The U.S. Department of Education proposal is aiming at improving outcomes for students by prioritizing "programs that include a comprehensive redesign of the school day, week, or year, that promote schools as the center of their communities, or that partner with community organizations" (U.S. Department of Education, 2010a, p. 7). Investment will be made in new models that "keep students safe, supported, and healthy both in and out of school, and that support strategies to better engage families and community members in their children's education" (U.S. Department of Education, 2010a, p. 7).

Reflections on the Adequate Yearly Progress/Student Achievement Crisis

Education reform in the form of powerful NCLB legislation or the pending ESEA (NCLB Reauthorization) and education incentives such as Race to the Top sends a clear message to educators: student learning must improve so that America can remain globally competitive. Secretary of Education Arne Duncan made this point in reference to the National Association of Educational Progress (NAEP) reading and math scores:

> Today's results once again show that the achievement of American students isn't growing fast enough. After modest gains in recent years, 4th grade reading scores are flat and 8th grade scores were up just one point. The achievement gap didn't narrow by a statistically significant amount in either grade. Like the NAEP 2009 math scores released last fall, the reading scores demonstrate that students aren't making the progress necessary to compete in the global economy. . . . We shouldn't be satisfied with these results. By this and many other measures, our students aren't on a path to graduate high school ready to succeed in college and the workplace. (U.S. Department of Education, 2010b, p. 1).

The NCLB legislation has enacted accountability measures to ensure that no student is left behind academically. By the school year 2013–2014, 100% of students in schools across America must demonstrate proficiency on state standardized tests. Since 2002, schools across America have thus been fixated on one thing—how to make AYP. The specific formula for making AYP may be broadened with ESEA, but districts, schools, and teachers will still be called upon to produce bottom-line results—significant and sustained increases in student learning. This is the crisis many schools face.

The Solution: Proven Correlate Strategies

Chapter 2 introduces the seven correlates of effective schools that are supported by decades of research. It describes studies that link the correlates to student achievement, including one author's landmark study that links AYP scores to the correlates. Chapters 3–9 distill the strategies gleaned from the ongoing case studies, surveys, interviews, vignettes, perspectives, and research to introduce powerful practices that highly effective educators use to improve student learning and help schools make the grade. Educators at all levels who cultivate these strategies can be assured that no child is left behind and that each child receives a world-class education. You are the key to their tomorrow.

CHAPTER REFLECTION

1. Do you agree or disagree with Secretary of Education Duncan's statement that "our students aren't on a path to graduate high school ready to succeed in college and the workplace" (U.S. Department of Education, 2010b, p. 1)? Explain your response, and give specific examples.

2. Given the case study scenarios and data, how would you account for Pine Grove making AYP and John D. Floyd failing to make AYP? Give two or three specific reasons to support your answer.

3. In your opinion, what is the driving force behind NCLB? ESEA? Give two or three explicit examples.

4. Explain AYP in your own words. What happens to schools when they fail to make AYP? Give one or two examples.

5. What is Differentiated Accountability? Do you agree or disagree with it?

6. The U.S. Department of Education has identified five priorities detailed in the Blueprint for Reform. Do you agree or disagree with these priorities? Give a rationale for each priority.

7. Explain the purpose of the Race to the Top competition. Will this help or hinder student learning? Explain your response, giving two or three specific examples.

Patricia Doyle, fourth-grade teacher and Teacher of the Year at Pine Grove Elementary School, explains that developing collaborative teams and mentoring teachers were key components that contributed to Pine Grove Elementary's success:

As teachers we strive to develop caring relationships with our students in order to meet their needs. Even as veteran professionals, sometimes we need a little help meeting our own classroom needs. Our "I'm there for you" message routinely encourages and supports students, yet we fail to recognize this support can come from a caring, committed colleague who is willing to provide whatever tools are necessary to help maximize our effectiveness as a teacher. Being there for a teacher is the cornerstone of mentoring, because the challenges of classroom teaching can occur at any time—first year or tenth year. These challenges can range from simple practical issues such as forms or paperwork, best solving classroom management issues, or more complex instructional strategies to best suit student needs.

Creating a sense of comfort and community is my first priority when mentoring a colleague. Being approachable, offering a cup of coffee or snack, goes a long way towards opening dialogue and discussion. Your caring smile and congenial atmosphere provide acceptance of your colleague's uniqueness without them fearing rejection for needing assistance. An open-door policy for questions or classroom observations can provide the support or inspiration for success. In other cases, teaching a collaborative lesson or just sharing a resource may be all that is needed. I've personally sat in on lessons, shared new technology, and have gone as far as helping move/set up a classroom.

I would encourage all teachers to be mentors in some way. My advice is that regardless of your method, when you share knowledge along with your experiences, don't forget to share what hasn't worked. Laughing through your own struggles reinforces that mistakes do make you a better teacher. Your own transparency and quest for learning models a commitment to best practices. Therefore, I'll also suggest due diligence for further reading, investigating, or professional development to be up-to-date on the current trends. This way you can share the information that you have, and hopefully another teacher on staff will share something with you. This way you are all mentoring and collaborating with one another.

Also, I would suggest always have a good attitude. Generally, I smile and remind my colleague to relax and breathe because whether tomorrow or a week from then—lesson plans, data, parents, ideas, or simply venting— "I'm there for them." Confident and secure, my colleague can now walk back to their classroom more optimistic and energized to approach this or any other classroom challenge, because they know there's a caring professional "there for them." That's what it's all about as teachers—being there for each other and working together as a team.

What Makes a School Effective in Improving Student Achievement?

We can, whenever and wherever we choose, successfully teach all children whose schooling is of interest to us. We already know more than we need to do that. Whether or not we do it must finally depend on how we feel about the fact that we haven't so far.

—R.R. Edmonds (1979b, p. 35)

I [Martin Ratcliffe] returned to public school teaching from private school administration in 2002 for a 5-year period while completing my doctorate in educational leadership. I noted that each year our school (and school district) completed a survey on the correlates of effective schools. I began to research the correlates (seven in all) and found out that they were backed by decades of research. The research showed that effective schools had a strong presence of the correlates, but not so in ineffective schools. By this time, NCLB was in force, accompanied by the mandate for AYP that schools had to make. If AYP scores were also considered to be indications of a school's effectiveness, perhaps there was a relationship between the correlates of effective schools and student academic achievement as measured by AYP scores. This idea took root and grew into a full dissertation study.

I had the unique experience of being a full-time teacher by day and a fully involved researcher in the evenings and very early mornings. The result was a completed study that was unique in looking at the relationship between the correlates of effective schools and AYP scores. My study corroborated the findings in other similar studies between the correlates and student achievement pointing to the critical importance of the seven key correlates in effective schools.

This chapter will discuss the seven correlates, provide supportive research, and take a closer look at the results of my own study. The next seven chapters focus on each correlate separately, sharing case studies, vignettes,

19

perspectives, interviews, and research, and culminate in sharing practical research-supported and experientially tested correlate strategies that will help teachers and schools to increase student learning and improve AYP scores.

CORRELATES

Lezotte (2002) notes a distinction between first-generation and second-generation correlates. In keeping with the current focus on school proficiency, we as authors have selected the terms *proficient* to represent first-generation schools and *advanced* to represent second-generation schools. In our understanding, proficient schools follow the "letter of the law" by enforcing the presence of correlates, whereas correlates are an integral part of the culture of an advanced school. (Reference will be made to these distinctions in the discussions of each correlate in Chapters 3–9.) Table 2.1 lists the seven correlates and briefly describes the differences between their presence in a proficient and an advanced school.

Backdrop to the Correlates

Congress made a request for the important Coleman study, which resulted in the report titled *Equality of Education Opportunity* (Coleman et al., 1966) at about the same time as the historic 1965 ESEA was passed. Congress had made a request that this study be completed in response to the 1964 Civil

Table 2.1.   Proficient (first-generation) and advanced (second-generation) correlates

Correlate	Proficient (first generation) Letter of law	Advanced (second generation) Spirit of the law
Instructional Leadership	Mission communicated—all	Dispersed leadership
Clear and Focused Mission	Mastery—low-level skills Teaching for all	Higher-level; learning for all Results oriented
Safe and Orderly Environment	Absence of specific undesirable behaviors	Increased emphasis on certain desirable behaviors
Climate of High Expectations	Institution for instruction Staff believes mastery—all	Institution for learning Ensure mastery; reteaching
Frequent Monitoring of Student Progress	Frequent/varied assessment of pupil progress	Strategic technology = closer monitoring of learning
Positive Home–School Relations	Parents cognizant of mission and support it	Parents and teachers partners—build trust, communication
Opportunity to Learn and Student Time on Task	Teacher-directed; essential skills instruction	Interdisciplinary teaching— organized abandonment

Source: Lezotte (1991).

Rights Act (PL 88-352) to assess the distribution of educational resources by race, and then to generally assess equality of education in the nation's public schools (Stringfield, 2004).

Coleman Camp—Schools Do Not Make a Difference Studies spawned as a direct or indirect result of the request made by Congress fall into two research camps that can be called the "Coleman camp" (after the Coleman study and corroborating studies) and the "Edmonds camp" (after the late Dr. Ron Edmonds, because he was regarded by many as a key voice for effective schools). The body of research studies initiated by Coleman and colleagues (1966) and corroborated in studies by Jensen (1969) and Jencks et al. (1972) believed that schools make little difference to academic achievement. They believed that the effects of school were outweighed by home environmental factors, suggesting that schools did not matter. For example, Coleman noted that "schools bring little influence to bear on a child's background and general social context" (Coleman et al., 1966, p. 325). The impact of the Coleman report and subsequent studies was far reaching and dominated educational thinking and public policy during the late 1960s and 1970s.

Edmonds Camp—Schools Do Make a Difference Reaction to the Coleman camp spawned an *effective schools movement* in the Edmonds camp that has lasted almost 4 decades. According to noted school reformer Ben Birdsell (personal communication, June 17, 2005), the effective schools movement is one of the driving forces behind the federal government's NCLB Act of 2001. Clearly, researchers in the Edmonds camp believed that schools and teachers do make a difference to student achievement.

It is from this body of research in the Edmonds camp that characteristics of unusually effective schools emerged. These characteristics were refined over time to become known as *the correlates of effective schools.*

An Overview of Key Studies

Studies in the 1970s, 1980s, and 1990s by effective school researchers such as Edmonds (1979a, 1979b); Weber (1971); Brookover, Beady, Flood, Schweitzer, and Wisebaker (1979); Mortimore, Sammons, Stoll, Lewis, and Ecob (1988); Rutter (1983); Rutter, Maughan, Ouston, and Smith (1979); Teddlie and Stringfield (1993); and Levine and Lezotte (1990) held that schools *do* matter and have an effect on students that is independent of home background variables.

Scheerens and Bosker (1997), Kyriakides and Luyten (2006), Creemers (2002), and other school effects researchers have sought to identify the absolute effects of schooling absent home background variables. Reviews on the link between correlates of effective schools and student

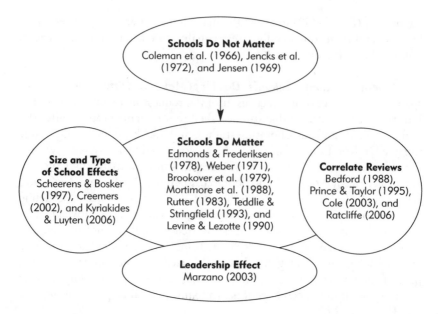

Figure 2.1.   Overview of key studies on the role of schools in academic achievement.

achievement were advanced by Bedford (1988), Prince and Taylor (1995), Cole (2003), and Ratcliffe (2006), while numerous splinter studies point to the support of individual correlates, in particular the effect of leadership on student achievement, as purported by Marzano (2003). For a summary of key studies that examine the effects of schools on academic success, see Figure 2.1.

Empirical Research

This section digs into the research archives and takes a closer look at some foundational correlate-supportive studies.

Correlates of Effective Schools and Student Achievement   One cornerstone study that has had an impact on the correlates is that by Weber (1971), who conducted studies in four exemplary inner-city schools (two in New York City, one in Kansas City, and one in Los Angeles) showing that it is possible for inner-city schools to teach reading successfully. He identified five characteristics common to each of the four schools: 1) strong instructional leadership, 2) high expectations for students, 3) an orderly and pleasant environment, 4) frequent monitoring of pupil progress, and 5) a strong emphasis on students learning basic reading skills, thereby paving the way for others to build on and refine effective school characteristics.

Edmonds (1979a, 1979b) was a forerunner among effective school researchers and the first to identify "tangible and indispensable characteristics of effective schools" (Edmonds, 1979b, p. 33) (or correlates) as follows: 1) strong administrative leadership, 2) climate of expectation, 3) orderly school atmosphere, 4) an emphasis on basic skills, and 5) frequent monitoring of student progress.

Other key studies also concluded that other school factors besides home background were correlated to student achievement. For example, Brookover et al. (1979) demonstrated the importance of the school social environment in relation to student achievement. Only a small proportion of the between-school variance in achievement was explained by socioeconomic status and racial composition after the effect of school climate was removed. According to Brookover et al., the highest correlation with student achievement was with the student sense of academic futility.

Lezotte, Edmonds, and Ratner (1974) identified and analyzed 20 city schools that were instructionally effective for children who were poor and/or from minority groups. They compared the mean mathematics and reading scores of these schools with citywide norms to identify effective and ineffective schools. The results of this study indicated that elementary school instructional effectiveness was not predicated on family background. Edmonds and Frederiksen (1978) reached a similar conclusion when they identified 55 effective schools in their reanalysis of the 1966 EEOS Coleman study. They found that the large differences between effective and ineffective schools could not be attributed to social class and background but to certain school factors correlated to student achievement.

Mortimore et al. (1988) conducted a longitudinal study in London in which they followed a group of 2,000 pupils from 50 junior schools randomly selected from the 636 schools in the authority. In harmony with Edmonds, Brookover, Weber, and other effective schools researchers, Mortimore et al. (1988) showed that "schools, rather than background, have the greatest influence on levels of pupil progress" (p. 280). They identified the following 12 factors of schools that contribute positively to school effect and offered them as a framework within which the various partners in the life of the school—head teacher and staff, parents and pupils, and governors— can operate:

1. Purposeful leadership of the staff by the head teacher,
2. The involvement of the deputy head,
3. The involvement of teachers,
4. Consistency among teachers,
5. Structured sessions,
6. Intellectually challenging teaching,
7. The work-centered environment,
8. Limited focus within sessions,

   9. Maximum communication between teachers and pupils,
  10. Record keeping,
  11. Parental involvement, and
  12. Positive climate. (p. 250)

Rutter et al. (1979) conducted a longitudinal study of inner-London primary school students as they entered 12 secondary schools. The study revealed similar findings to those reported by Brookover et al. (1979) in demonstrating that "other school factors were significantly associated with pupil success, even after the composition of the student body had been taken into account" (Rutter, 1983, p. 19).

Another key study supporting the Edmonds camp was the Louisiana School Effectiveness Study (LSES), reported by Teddlie and Stringfield (1993), which began in 1980 and lasted through the 1980s. The purpose of the study was to determine whether there were schools that were differentially effective in their ability to educate students. The overall results replicated Brookover's major conclusion that schools do make a difference.

Levine and Lezotte (1990) presented a synthesis of research on unusually effective schools based mostly on case studies in which unusually effective schools were compared with ineffective schools. Although they are strongly supportive of the correlates of effective schools, they cautioned that the correlates should be seen as prerequisites and not as guarantees of school success.

School Effects Researchers

Table 2.2 shows a comparison between studies completed by school effects researchers Scheerens and Bosker (1997) and Kyriakides and Luyten (2006). Both studies point to schools having an effect on student academic achievement. Scheerens and Bosker found that, "on average, schools account for 19% of the achievement differences between students (for gross effects, that is without the partialling out of other variables) and for 8% when adjusting for initial differences between students" (p. 77). Kyriakides and Luyten (2006) found that "schooling accounts for more than 50% of the cognitive development of students" (p. 4). These studies show that schools make a difference.

Correlate Studies

Table 2.3 hones in on three key studies that show a significant relationship between the correlates and student achievement. Overall, the correlates account for between about 30%–51% of the variance on student academic achievement. Each of the studies identified the Positive Home–School Relations correlate as the number one predictor of student academic achieve-

Table 2.2. Overview of key school effects

Researchers (year)	Scheerens and Bosker (1997)	Kyriakides and Luyten (2006)
State/country	International	International
Number of participants	Meta analyses—168 studies	8 countries
Data source	Qualitative reviews Quantitative research synthesis	TIMMS, PISA
Methodology	5 empirical studies International comparison analysis	N/A
Analysis	Quantitative analysis	Regression discontinuity Multi-level analysis
Primary effect	Parental involvement	N/A
Secondary effect	Educational leadership	N/A
Overall effect	19% gross 8% partial	> 50% cognitive growth

Key: TIMMS, Trends in Mathematics and Science Achievement (Boston College, Lynch School of Education, 1999); PISA, Program for International Student Achievement (National Center for Education Statistics, n.d.).

ment. One study by Prince and Taylor (1995) (not included in Table 2.3) indicated mixed results. They concluded that "the real benefits of the presence of the Correlates may not be reflected in gain scores on standardized achievement tests, particularly over a two-year period" (p. 24). Overall, correlate studies by Bedford (1988), Cole (2003), and Ratcliffe (2006) indicate a clear and significant relationship between the correlates of effective schools and student academic achievement.

Supportive Correlate Studies

Table 2.4 shows four key studies that found a relationship between the presence of the correlates and student academic achievement. One success story from Table 2.4 is of a school district that infused the correlates into everyday school life. In 1991, Brazosport Independent School District in Texas received its state-mandated "report card," and 9 of 19 schools received the lowest designated scores. According to Anderson (2002), the district then implemented an eight-step process based on the integration of effective schools research (correlates) and total quality management and continuous improvement with careful attention to implement the Plan-Do-Check-Act cycle. In less than 10 years, the Brazosport district had earned the exemplary school district distinction, meaning that 90% or more of the students in the district and within each identified subgroup had achieved proficiency on the state exams in reading, mathematics, and writing.

Table 2.3.   Correlates and student achievement

Researcher (year)	Bedford (1988)	Cole (2003)	Ratcliffe (2006)
State	Georgia	Louisiana	Florida
Number of participants	70 middle schools	13 elementary magnet schools	19 schools (10 elementary, 4 middle, 4 high, 1 alternative)
Years of data	1 year	1 year	3 years
Test	Georgia Criterion-Referenced Competency Test (CCRT; Georgia Department of Eduation, n.d.)	Iowa Test of Basic Skills (ITBS; Iowa Department of Education, n.d.) + Louisiana Educational Assessment Program (LEAP; Louisiana Department of Education, n.d.)	Adequate yearly progress (AYP; U.S. Department of Education, n.d.-c)
Survey	Connecticut School Effectiveness Questionnaire (CSEQ; Villanova, Gauthier, Proctor, & Shoemaker, 1981)	More Effective Schools Staff Survey (Cardella & Sudlow, 2000)	Effective School Correlates (ESC)
Analysis	Regression	Regression	Regression
Primary effect	Home–School Relations	Home–School Relations	Parent and Community Involvement
Secondary effect	Instructional Leadership	Instructional Leadership -ve (Inverse relationship to student achievement)	Collaboration Among Staff -ve (Inverse relationship to student achievement)
Overall effect	> 30 % variance	39.1% of variance	51.2% of AYP variance

Key: -ve, negative.

RESEARCH SUMMARY

Research has identified seven key factors identified in multiple studies that are correlated to exceptional student achievement. These factors, known as *correlates,* are

1.   Positive Home–School Relations
2.   Opportunity to Learn and Student Time on Task
3.   Climate of High Expectations
4.   Clear and Focused Mission
5.   Frequent Monitoring of Student Progress

Table 2.4. Correlates and student achievement—supportive studies

Researcher(s) (year)	Cawelti and Protheroe (2001)	Anderson (2002)	Keedy and McDonald (2006)	Nesselrodt (2006)
State/country	United States	Texas	Kentucky	Pennsylvania
Number of participants	4 high-achieving, low-income school districts	In 1991, 9 of 19 schools with the lowest scores; eight-step process based on the integration of effective schools research, and total quality management (TQM), and continuous improvement with attention to implement the Plan-Do-Check-Act cycle	3 low socioeconomic schools that consistently surpassed state benchmarks	1 high school with English as a Second language program ranked "Effective" per the No Child Left Behind Act of 2001 (PL 107-110)
Analysis	Qualitative	Quantitative/Qualitative	Qualitative	Qualitative
Overall effect	Found compelling presence of the correlates OHCFISH	≤ 10 years > 90% proficiency for the correlates OHCFISH	Displayed presence of HCFI	Found presence of correlates OFI

Key: O, Opportunity to Learn and Student time on Task; H, Climate of High Expectations; C, Clear and Focused Mission; F, Frequent Monitoring of Student Progress; I, Instructional Leadership; S, Safe and Orderly Environment; H, Positive Home–School Relations.

6. Instructional Leadership
7. Safe and Orderly Environment

Effective schools have been found to have a strong correlate presence. Three key correlate studies (including the author's) have demonstrated a significant relationship between the correlates and student academic achievement. The author's study is unique in that it demonstrates the relationship between the correlates and AYP.

ADEQUATE YEARLY PROGRESS/CORRELATE STUDY

This study utilized a quantitative research perspective and a correlational research type. It was designed to aid educational leaders in utilizing effective school correlates with greater precision in order to meet the federally mandated AYP accountability requirements.

Method

The purpose of the study (Ratcliffe, 2006) was to investigate whether a relationship existed between correlates of effective schools and school effectiveness scores as determined by aggregate AYP measures. Figure 2.2 provides a schematic for the author's method. First, 3 years of aggregate correlate survey data were collected for the 19 schools in the author's school district. (Correlate survey data were gathered on the seven correlates plus one extra correlate included on the survey by the school district. Data were gathered for the 2003, 2004, and 2005 school years.) This amounted to correlate data from about 4,400 surveys. Three years of corresponding AYP data were also collected on each of the 19 schools. Using SPSS software (Brace, Kemp, & Snelgar, 2006), a forward step regression analysis of the data was completed, enabling the identification of the correlates that predicted AYP scores.

Uniqueness of the Study

A number of studies (mentioned in the research noted earlier) have looked at the relationship between a host of school variables and student academic achievement. In addition, three correlate studies have looked at the relationship between preidentified correlates of effective schools and student academic achievement. The author's study was titled *A Study of the Relationship Between the Correlates of Effective Schools and Aggregate Adequate Yearly Progress (AYP) Scores* (Ratcliffe, 2006). It was unique in that it specifically looked at the relationship between the correlates and student academic achievement as measured by AYP scores, NCLB's high-stakes accountability measure of an effective school. The null hypothesis was that there is no significant relationship between the correlates of effective schools and aggregate AYP school effectiveness scores.

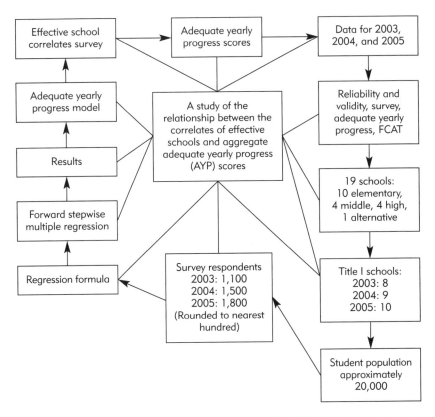

Figure 2.2. Adequate yearly progress/correlate study method. (*Key: FCAT, Florida Comprehensive Assessment Test* [Florida Department of Education, Bureau of K-12 Assessment, 2010].)

Summary of Key Findings

Figure 2.3 shows the "model of best fit" when the eight correlate variables were entered into a forward stepwise multiple regression. This model includes the most significantly contributing predictors: 1) PHSR (Positive Home–School Relations), which accounted for 39.5% of the AYP variance; 2) CAS (Collaboration Among Staff [school district correlate]), which contributed an additional 7.0%; and 3) FMSP (Frequent Monitoring of Student Progress), which contributed an additional 4.7% to the variance, for a total of 51.2% of the variance on the criterion AYP variable. All three beta coefficients were significant. In other words, each predictor variable contributed significantly in affecting the criterion variable. There were no other significant relationships remaining among other correlate variables and the criterion AYP variable. An ANOVA (analysis of variance) revealed that this model was significant at $p < .0005$, an alpha level far below that of $p < .05$; thus, this model appears to be a very good model.

Predictor variable	Beta	P
PHSR	.546	p = 0.009
CAS	–.676	p < 0.0005
FMSP	.646	p = 0.018

Adjusted R square = .512; $F_{3,51}$ = 19.896;
p < .0005 (using the stepwise method).
Significant variables are shown above.

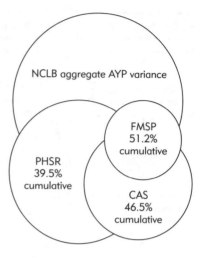

Figure 2.3. Key findings summary. The key adequate yearly progress (AYP) predictor correlates in this study were Positive Home-School Relations (PHSR), Collaboration Among Staff (CAS) (inverse relationship), and Frequent Monitoring of Student Progress (FMSP). (Key: NCLB, No Child Left Behind Act of 2001 [PL 107-110].)

Discussion of the Results

The null hypothesis could be rejected, because there was a significant relationship between the correlates and aggregate AYP scores.

The study showed that the number one predictor of AYP scores was the correlate Positive Home–School Relations. This was a very important finding, as it was significantly correlated with AYP scores and it was also the number one predictor of student academic achievement in the Bedford (1988) and Cole (2003) correlate studies. Similarly, numerous other studies have identified the home–school influence as the number one predictor of student achievement, including Scheerens and Bosker (1997) in their meta-analysis of 168 studies.

The second AYP predictor was the school district correlate added to the survey, namely Collaboration Among Staff. Interestingly, there was an inverse relationship between this correlate and AYP scores. In other words, the more teachers collaborated, the worse the AYP scores become. At first glance, this finding appears to be counterintuitive, given the research to the contrary. However, it may perhaps be explained by a phenomenon noted with alarm by researchers Daly and Chrispeels (2006): NCLB's threat- and sanction-driven methods, they claimed, are increasing stress levels and "potentially causing a threat-rigid response" (p. 1). Perhaps overstressed teachers are not interested in "another" meeting, hence the inverse relationship. Certainly, more research is needed in this area. The third predictor correlate was Frequent Monitoring of Student Progress.

The remaining predictor correlates in all three correlate studies (including the author's) varied, pointing to the context-specific nature of schools. The Positive Home–School Relations correlate is consistently the number one predictor of student academic achievement, but subsequent predictors vary according to the school context. This makes sense. Schools are unique and have unique needs, and may need to cultivate certain correlates more than others. However, the research has shown that *all* of the correlates are important, and they are the hallmark of effective schools.

So What? Implications of the Findings

The results of the author's AYP/correlate study allow schools to use correlates of effective schools with greater precision to meet AYP contextualized for their particular locale. There are several other important implications:

1. All federally funded schools in the United States are required to make AYP or face consequences.
2. This research study aids in the identification of correlates that are predictors of AYP.
3. This study includes an understanding of the rank and strength of the relationship between certain correlates and AYP.
4. This is a research-based, data-driven study that is broadly generalizable.
5. This research model should facilitate increased precision leadership when each school or school region replicates the study, incorporates the study results into its School Improvement Plan (SIP), and strategically cultivates the presence of identified high-yield predictor correlates.
6. The identification and cultivation of these high-yield and context-specific predictor correlates should improve student academic achievement across delineated subgroups, resulting in improved AYP scores.
7. This study adds to the knowledge base in educational leadership by providing a statistical research base that strengthens the link between effective school correlates and student achievement while uniquely contributing to the correlate/AYP research.
8. This quantitative study establishes a statistical research base needed to support a widely accepted body of anecdotal and qualitative research.
9. This study opens the field for additional quantitative research on the relationship between the correlates of effective schools and aggregate AYP scores.

SUMMARY

The Coleman report of 1966 concluded that schools do not make a difference, saying "schools bring little influence to bear on a child's background and general social context" (Coleman et al., 1966, p. 325). The impact of the Coleman report and subsequent studies was far reaching, but they spawned studies with contrary results from such researchers as Edmonds and Frederiksen (1978), Brookover et al. (1979), Mortimore et al. (1988), Rutter (1983), Teddlie and Stringfield (1993), and Levine and Lezotte (1990), among others, who paved the way in effective schools research. Edmonds was a forerunner among effective school researchers and the first to identify "tangible and indispensable characteristics of effective schools" [or correlates] (Edmonds, 1979b, p. 33) These characteristics were identified in multiple studies over time and refined to become the correlates of effective schools.

The correlates are not isolated from one another, but are rather interdependent (Lezotte, 2002). The notion is that by improving key correlates, other correlates improve too. Clearly, the correlates are not mere options for an effective school. They are a very important part of raising student achievement in schools. In fact, they are the leading organizational and contextual indicators of a school that have been shown to influence student learning: According to Lezotte, "The extent to which the correlates are in place in a school has a dramatic, positive effect on student achievement" (p. 24). Correlates, then, are keys to raising student academic achievement.

Understanding the critical relationship between correlates in general and student learning is an important first step. An awareness of the unique positive relationship between the correlates and AYP scores is an important second step. Operationalizing, or putting into practice, each of the seven correlates is a critical third step. Chapters 3–9 each focus on a separate correlate and bring the reader research-based and real-time practical strategies that district administrators, principals, and teachers can implement to play their part in ensuring that every student—regardless of socioeconomic status, ethnic origin, religion, or exceptionality—makes AYP and that schools make the grade. And operationalizing the correlates yields correlate solutions to the AYP/achievement crisis.

CHAPTER REFLECTION

1. Do you agree or disagree with Edmonds when he writes, "We can, whenever and wherever we choose, successfully teach all children whose schooling is of interest to us" (1979b, p. 35)? Support your response with two or three research-based examples.

2. In your opinion, how reliable are the correlates? Can they boost achievement? Support your answer with two or three examples from the research and your own experience.

3. Compare and contrast the Coleman and Edmonds research camps. What is each camp saying? Which research camp do you support? Give two or three reasons why you support this camp.

4. Coleman noted that "schools bring little influence to bear on a child's background and general social context" (Coleman et al., 1966, p. 325). Do you agree or disagree with the statement? Give two or three specific reasons.

5. Summarize what the research says about the correlates and student achievement. Include three or four specific references.

6. Explain what the author's AYP/correlate study shows about the relationship between the correlates and AYP scores. What is the significance of this study in regard to helping schools improve student learning? Support your answer with three or four research-based statements from the study.

7. What is meant by the operationalization of the correlates? Why would this be of benefit to student learning and AYP scores? Give three or four specific reasons.

Positive Home–School Relations Correlate

with Samuel R. Bennett

The American family is the rock on which a solid education can and must be built.

—Richard W. Riley (1994, para. 4),
former U.S. Secretary of Education

Correlate Definition In *proficient schools,* parents are cognizant of the school's basic mission, support it, and are provided opportunities of involvement to aid the school in achieving its mission. In *advanced schools,* parents and teachers must come together as partners in an authentic relationship that builds the trust and communication required to address issues of mutual concern. (Lezotte, 1997; Lezotte & McKee, 2002)

Our state school grade had been released showing that once again J.D. Floyd had made an A. However, the principal and I [Melissa Harts] wanted to explain to parents what the disaggregated data showed per grade level and what areas we needed to work on to strengthen student skills. We also wanted to give them strategies that could be used at home to support instruction in the classroom. Therefore, we decided to step out on a limb and have data review nights for each level hoping that the parents would be interested enough to attend and partner with us in helping their children make learning gains.

The day before the data review parent night presentation, the teachers and I met to review our discussion points. Some of them said to me, "Dr. Harts, we do not think the parents will come." I remember reassuring them by saying that we had done everything possible to advertise the event, but deep down inside, truth be told, I did not believe the parents would come either.

We had put a reminder in our school bulletin, posted it on our school web site, advertised it on our marquee board in the parking lot, and sent a note home in each student's backpack. It was an important meeting for us, but we kept asking ourselves if it would seem as important to the parents. As the middle school assistant principal, I had planned the obligatory Power-Point presentation explaining the state's testing requirements, the grade-level expectations, and a synopsis of the curriculum for the tested areas for third and fourth grades. We required the teachers from each grade level to attend and had representation from our administration and school leadership team. The reading resource coach was there to present the part of the presentation that emphasized the correlation with the new reading series; the math resource coach had the other part of the presentation along with the job of demonstrating some of the math manipulatives that could be used at home. We also had a display table of student work, at-home practice sheets, and a list of online homework resources and study guides. The team leader was also there to answer any questions specific to the grade level or classroom instructional strategies. And, of course, we had the required coffee, tea, and pastry table, elaborately decorated as if we were expecting it to be photo-graphed for a layout in Martha Stewart Living *magazine.*

Our goal was to demystify the test-taking requirements, arm parents with enough information to be prepared to assist their students at home, and bridge the communication gap between school and home that had grown so wide in the previous year of pointing fingers due to the stress of accountability. To our relief, at the scheduled 6 p.m. hour, streams of parents filled the cafeteria—and to our amazement, they stayed until the end of our presentation, asked pertinent questions, and some remained for coffee and pastries and an opportunity to speak individually to the teachers.

It was not the food that brought in the parent crowd. They were hungry for information on how to help their children and, in turn, support what teachers were doing in the classrooms. That night, they proved to us that as a group, parents do care; they will take the time out of their busy schedules, and if we build a bridge across the communication divide, they will come. That night, we all—administrators, teachers, and parents—gained a new respect for each other and the role we all had to play in ensuring that our *students succeeded and made demonstrable learning gains. That night set a precedent for how and what we communicated to parents from that point forward. We made sure that every year we held data review meetings, opened our classrooms for parent night discussions on data scores, and included data reports and analysis in our administrative parent–teacher conferences. We concentrated on providing parent nights for math and language arts, because our standardized scores were lower in those core areas. As the administrator over language arts, I made sure that parents were aware of after-school tutoring sessions, knew the tested state standards in fourth and eighth grades, and more importantly, had teacher and parent meetings on individual students where parents received prescriptive strategies for their child. The end result was that we saw an increase from 77% of the students making standards in writing from the year before (2005–2006) to 87% making standards in the 2006–2007 school year. Our language arts cur-*

riculum did not change, nor did our instructional practices. The main factors attributed to this increase were our individualized approach to student learning and our increased communication and participation from the parents.

Here's the kicker to the story: We then spiraled our strategy throughout the grade levels. We required parent data team meetings, especially for the grades preceding standardized tested areas. For example, in language arts, we required teams to meet with the parents in third and seventh grade so that those parents were introduced to the concepts expected in the following grade, had ample time to do practice exercises with their students, and were well aware of their child's individual progress in writing at least 2 years before the statewide exam.

IMPORTANCE OF POSITIVE HOME–SCHOOL RELATIONS

The number one predictor of student academic success as measured by the all important AYP scores is the Positive Home–School Relations correlate (Ratcliffe, 2006). Cole (2003) also identified this correlate as the number one predictor of student academic achievement, as did Scheerens and Bosker (1997) in their meta-analysis on school effects. U.S. Education Secretary Arne Duncan highlighted these points by describing parents as teachers and noting the importance of parent–school partnerships (National Public Radio, 2010).

A study conducted by Houtenville and Conway (2008) showed that parental involvement has a strong, positive effect on student achievement. In a 2003 report, *Parsing the Achievement Gap II*, the Educational Testing Service reported national trends between students of diverse racial and socioeconomic backgrounds (Educational Testing Service, 2003). The report listed 14 factors that have been linked to student achievement. Not surprisingly, nine of those factors related to a child's parents and home environment. This is not difficult to comprehend, because the more children see parents around schools (especially their own parents), the more they realize the importance of school. Students deduce that a parent being in a school makes it a viable place be-

Parent Perspective

When parents are involved in the day-to-day activities of their child's school, the children are able to perform better academically, not miss as many days, and have better social skills. . . . Parental involvement also doesn't mean just moms. Dads are important too! Young boys need the influence of a male, and when they are involved with the child at school, that child succeeds. There are many ways to be involved, such as setting time aside each day to talk about school activities and what they learned that day. Help them have a scheduled homework time. Being an involved parent is a key component to the success of a child.

—Parent and Chairperson of Communications and Public Relations, Parent Teacher Association (PTA)

cause "my parents come here to help and support on their day off" or "my parents care enough about me to want to be a part of what I am doing and to make a contribution to an important place of learning." For some students, a parent's presence is a reminder that best behavior is expected and that they must pay attention to what the teacher is trying to convey. Whatever message a student takes from a parent's presence in the school or involvement in his or her child's learning process, the parent's participation makes that needed difference. As Fullan (1997) stated, "Nothing motivates a child more than when learning is valued by schools and families/community working together in partnership. . . . These forms of involvement do not happen by accident or even by invitation. They happen by explicit strategic intervention" (as cited in Blankstein, 2004, p. 167).

On the contrary, the lack of parental involvement leaves a gaping hole in the foundation of education, affecting not only the child but educators as well. Although teachers may not readily admit this at every parent conference, they *need* parents to help. Many times, parents come in with a barrage of questions that all start with "why." They look at the educator and expect an answer. Sometimes teachers do a wonderful job at coming up with those answers. However, the truth of the matter is that teachers do not have all of the answers. Sometimes parents have more answers than teachers do because they know their child, understand the dynamics at home, and have a history with that child that supersedes the information in the cumulative folder that is alphabetized in the front office or the synopsis given from the teacher the year before. The pieces of information that the parent provides offers clues and direction on how to teach that child, how to understand his or her needs, how to be better equipped in reaching that child so that he or she can reach his or her learning potential.

In addition, the parent also provides the necessary support at home to reinforce what teachers are doing in the classroom. Whether that support is curricular or behavioral in nature, it helps when parents ask their child for an agenda or organizer that has the child's homework assignments or asks their child for his or her latest test material to review at home. In addition, it helps when parents discuss assignments and projects or reinforce the expectation of good school behavior and respect for self and others in the classroom.

STRATEGIES FOR CREATING
EFFECTIVE HOME–SCHOOL RELATIONS

There are seven types of strategies that can improve the relationship between schools and families: communication, support, attendance, planning, engagement, implementation, and involvement. These strategies are important to consider at every level of a school, and everybody has a role to play.

What Highly Effective
Superintendents and District Administrators Do

The following are strategies that highly effective superintendents and district administrators use to *communicate* in order to increase positive relationships between home and school, superintendents, and districts.

- Stress the vision of a positive, collaborative home–school partnership to all constituents, particularly parents.
- Return parent telephone calls in a timely fashion.
- Draft parent-friendly policies that solicit and encourage positive parent involvement in the school.
- Clearly and frequently communicate district events, policies, academic status of schools, and availability of help for parents such as parenting workshops.

It is important for superintendents and district administrators to support efforts made to better the home–school connection by

- Supporting community programs and partnering with civic and private organizations
- Providing in-service support for principals and teachers regarding research-based and practical strategies aimed at bolstering positive home–school relations

Finally, superintendents and districts can show their support through their *attendance:* They can attend selected schools' PTA meetings and School Advisory Council meetings.

Parent Perspective

As the parent of a high school student, communication with the school is very important. I was able to contact any teacher via e-mail with my concern, and the teacher would respond when he/she was able.

—Parent of a high school student

What Highly Effective
Principals and School Administrators Do

Principals can encourage positive home–school relationships by using the following *communication* strategies.

- Maintain attractive, user-friendly, and updated web sites.
- Use every means and occasion to actively demonstrate that learning is highly valued and celebrated at your school.

Through *planning*, principals can increase opportunities to improve the home–school relationship.

- Plan "edutaining" (educational and entertaining) schoolwide events such as Data Night. Include a social and refreshment component.
- Strategically plan team-building opportunities between teachers, parents, and students.

Engaging families in the life of the school is an important aspect of creating positive home–school relationships.

- Welcome students' family members into the school setting. They want to learn too!
- Create opportunities for parent involvement, including all parents (where possible). Don't forget fathers!
- Build authentic relations with parents through fun social events, collaborative work days, and school projects that include parents and children.
- Consider institutionalizing parent hours as part of the school culture and exchange for meaningful privileges such as parental voice in the selection of their child's teacher.

Parent Perspective

Communicating with my son's teacher in multiple ways has helped in the clarification of assignments due, and what the teacher expects. Visiting during the school's open house allows my son to show off some of his displayed classwork, and allowed me to get an idea of my son's learning environment. E-mail, along with the web access to his grades and assignments, provide a means for answering various questions.

—Father of an elementary school student

Parent Perspective

Teachers can begin to cultivate opportunities and strategies for parent engagement both at school and at home. When a parent feels comfortable with the child's teacher(s) and in the classroom setting, then he or she will be more likely to get involved in other school activities as well as discuss and practice strategies that will best help the child to learn and succeed.

—Parent of secondary school student

What Highly Effective Teachers Do

Teachers play a major role in improving home–school relations. Some strategies they can use to *communicate* include the following:

- Treat parents respectfully as partners.
- Maintain regular and prompt communication with the home through notes, letters, telephone calls, web site links, and volunteer opportunities. (Keep all documentation.)

- Initiate positive, proactive communication with parents, including home visitation, before there are any issues.
- Begin and end parent meetings positively and professionally, communicating a caring attitude.

Teachers can *implement* their plans by strategically scheduling and planning for periodic parent–teacher conferences and involving the necessary personnel. The conferences should conclude with a clearly written action plan.

Finally, teachers can *involve* families by

- Creating opportunities for parental involvement, beginning with a back-to-school open house
- Involving the class in school events, and personally inviting parents to support them
- Involving parents in read-alouds at home and school
- Documenting parent–teacher meetings in a narrative format and soliciting parental input

SUPPORTIVE RESEARCH

Parental involvement is one of the few areas of education where there is widespread agreement. Large urban school districts consider parental involvement a requirement for improving the academic success for large numbers of mostly low-income students (Nichols-Solomon, 2001). Parent involvement improves student attitudes toward school, homework activity, school attendance, and academic achievement (Feuerstein, 2000).

Parent Perspective

It is very important to me, as a parent, to keep the communication lines open with all of my child's teachers. The primary way is the planner. Another way is the monthly newsletter. Last, is by the online grade book.

—Parent of an elementary school student

Parent Perspective

Schools, especially secondary ones, must strive to make parent involvement more user-friendly. It has to be more open-ended, allowing parents a variety of choices in which to get involved. Most parents only have small blocks of time to give. They don't want to feel like they are signing up for a life-sentence.

—Parent of secondary school student

Home Support Positively Affects Academics

Similar to most educators, Ban (2000) believes that education begins in the home. As homes are made true learning places, learning will improve in the schools. Parents need to become teachers in the home and start teaching children study skills. Cordry and Wilson (2004) wrote that parents should engage children in learning in the home prior to enrolling them in our schools. Students should arrive at the kindergarten doors with a solid foundation that has been built by the parents in the home, allowing teachers to build the educational house on top of that foundation. Riley (1994), former U.S. Secretary of Education, believes that the love of learning needs to be taught in the home in order for children to make a difference in the world. He asserted the following:

> I have seen examples all over this Nation where two-parent families, single parents, step-parents, grandparents, aunts and uncles are providing strong family support for their children to learn. If families teach the love of learning, it can make all the difference in the world to their children. (as cited in Family Involvement Partnership for Learning, 1998)

Several factors influence parental involvement, including a parent's confidence level, ethnicity, and educational and socioeconomic background. According to the Family Involvement Partnership for Learning (1998),

> Family involvement in education can mean: Reading a bedtime story to your preschool child . . . checking homework every night . . . getting involved in PTA . . . discussing your children's progress with teachers . . . voting in school board elections . . . helping your school to set challenging academic standards . . . limiting TV viewing to no more than two hours on school nights . . . getting personally involved in governing your school . . . becoming an advocate for better education in your community and state . . . and insisting on high standards of behavior for children.

Parent connectedness to school is stressed by the U.S. Department of Education (n.d.-b): "Parents need to feel connected to their children's school so they can provide encouragement to their offspring in pursuing their studies and advocate for them." Zellman and Waterman (1998) found that parents from minority groups were more involved in schools than parents from nonminority groups who were at the same socioeconomic level. Jacobson, Huffman, and Rositas de Cantu (1998) showed that Hispanic parents valued academic achievement and saw a need to help their children with learning at home. They did, however, believe they were less ready to help their children with reading and mathematics than Caucasian parents.

Hawes and Plourde (2005) conducted their study on parental involvement and the reading achievement of sixth grade students. They found many reasons why parents from ethnic minority groups did not participate in their children's education. They listed the following as barriers: "lack of education, feeling unwelcome, language difficulties, and time constraints" (p. 52). Their study found a slight correlation between the amount of parental involvement and the reading comprehension level of their children and determined that the students, themselves, could affect the amount of parental involvement happening in their education.

Tooling Teachers to Reach Parents

No matter what the factors are that influence the level of parental involvement, educators must be aware of them and continue to reach out to parents for their help and support. One of the most effective ways to improve the school's parental involvement plan is to convince teachers to buy into the program. The first line in communication for any effective parental involvement plan is the link between the parent and the teacher. Linek, Rasinski, and Harkins documented the need for the classroom teacher to support the parental involvement plan so that it will be effective: "Parental involvement appears to hold great potential for the improvement of literacy. Without the coordination and support of the classroom teacher, however, the effects of such involvement may not be maximized" (1997, p. 91).

Teachers need to understand that their communication with parents is pivotal, as it sets the tone for how the parents view the school and it provides the first building block in home–school communication. Teachers should recognize the importance of partnering with parents so that their students will benefit from the collaboration. Research by Winn, Hobbs, and Johnson (1998) shows that "parents believe teachers who encourage a great deal of parental involvement are better teachers" (p. 271). Kirschenbaum (1999) states that teachers who are more aggressive about involving parents usually are the better teachers. The more the teacher makes contact with the parent, the more the parent will participate (Feuerstein, 2000).

Christie (2005) wrote that schools should think in terms similar to President Kennedy's famous statement, "Ask not what your country can do for you; ask what you can do for your country." Her paradigm was, "Ask not what parents can do for the school, but what the school can do to ensure that the treatment of each student in each classroom meets the expectations that parents have for their children" (Christie, 2005, p. 646). Schools need to recognize that some parents have higher expectations for their children than the teachers do.

As the first line of communication with parents, teachers need the tools to foster a positive partnership. They need to be given the knowledge, time, resources, and recognition to get parents involved in the educational process of their children. One college teacher education program addressed the issue of tooling or training teachers in the area of parental involvement by teaching education majors the parental involvement plan. They found the following:

> Parental involvement is more than parents attending meetings and spending time at school. Parental involvement might also include the following: parents providing a home environment that supports education, schools communicating with parents about school programs and children's progress, parents supporting school events as spectators or volunteering in classrooms as aides, parents creating and imple-

menting a home learning environment, and parents participating in leadership roles and school governance. (Winn, Hobbs, & Johnson, 1998, p. 265)

Lazar, Broderick, Mastrilli, and Slostad (1999) recommend a more systematic plan to help teachers work with parents. This plan should start with teacher education programs and continue through in-service training programs for the development of veteran teachers. Unfortunately, although teachers, principals, and teacher educators understand the importance of parental involvement, most teacher education programs do not address this area with preservice teachers (Tichenor, 1998). This is an area that we need to examine as educators if we want to develop effective schools nationally.

Making the Parent Connection: Teamwork and Communication

A crucial component to the parent and school partnership is that parents need to feel as though the school wants them involved in the educational process of their children. The school needs to communicate that attitude to the parents so that they can feel that they are wanted and needed in making decisions about their child's learning and school environment. Naturally, students will benefit from this, because when students see their parents involved at the school, it makes them realize that they and their education are important. In addition, when the parent becomes involved in the educational process of the child, a team is formed with a valuable support system that works for the child's benefit. By feeling welcomed, parents are able to volunteer, which communicates to the child that they not only care about him or her but are also concerned with what is happening in the school (White, 1998).

Teachers, students, and school staff should have positive input in the process of getting parents more involved at the school. The national PTA has identified six elements of effective parent involvement programs. White summarized them as follows:

1. Communicating—Communication between home and school is regular, two-way, and meaningful.
2. Parenting—Parenting skills are promoted and supported.
3. Student Learning—Parents play an integral role in assisting student learning.
4. Volunteering—Parents are welcome in the school, and their support and assistance are sought.
5. School Decision Making and Advocacy—Parents are full partners in the decisions that affect children and families.
6. Collaborating with Community—Community resources are used to strengthen schools, families, and student learning. (1998, p. 8)

It is important to note here that the community at large can offer support to parents who are trying to participate in their child's education.

Making a connection with community members is helpful in expanding the support system for the parents, especially for those parents who feel somewhat helpless and estranged from the school culture. Some parents do not get involved in the school or community because of a language barrier. Involving the community in English classes for parents will improve and assist communications between parent, school, and community (Jacobson, Huffman, & Rositas de Cantu, 1998).

Schools need to become creative in making the parent connection. Many schools have gone to great lengths to make moms and dads more involved in the education of their children. Some schools bus families to school meetings, provide door prizes and dinner to families who attend, hold parent conferences at local fast food restaurants, or host monthly family nights that include pajama parties for students and their siblings (Curriculum Review, 2005). As the parent and school partnerships are developed, some barriers may persist. Schools should persist and make a strong, good faith effort to reach all parents, including those who are reluctant or who refuse to be involved. Once it is clear that certain parents just do not consider involvement a priority, then schools should focus energy on the interested parents. Curriculum Review (2005) put it this way:

> If the parent says, "It's my job to bear them and feed them, and it's the school's job to educate them," you're not going to get much help out of that parent. If the parent sees their job as a partner with the school to work together for the child's education, then they're going to be involved. (p. 11).

Parent–Teacher Conferences

Parents and teachers need to work together so that both are strengthened and improved through the collaborative partnership. Parent–teacher conferences are beneficial to nurturing parent involvement and collaboration. When teachers have that face-to-face meeting with the parent, it becomes much more personal. The ice has been broken, and the parent is more likely to become involved at the school. Parent–teacher conferences allow for the communication of student progress in an informal setting. Brandt (2003) came up with 12 steps to improve successful conferencing:

1. Begin with something positive.
2. Create a warm and inviting atmosphere.
3. Be straightforward.
4. Be sensitive.
5. Provide parents with details and a written account of comments.
6. Create a comprehensive evaluation including many different assessments.
7. Allow time for student's self-assessment.

8. Provide teacher evaluation of six academic areas (reading, language arts, spelling, math, social studies, and science).

9. Provide teacher evaluation of four behavior categories (organization, responsibility, conduct, and social skills).

10. Leave students out of the actual conference (but remain flexible, as some conferences may be enhanced by a student's presence).

11. Complete an action plan that becomes a student–parent contract.

12. Write a narrative of the conference.

Brandt's strategy could be a successful plan in the developmental approach to parent–teacher conferencing.

Parent–teacher conferencing can be the first line of open communication between teacher and parent. When the parent puts a face to the voice and recognizes that the teacher's goal is to help his or her child, the parent will respond in a positive way. As Bulach and Potter said, "Every educator knows the importance of parents' involvement in their children's education. In fact, a strong link between school and home is considered to be the greatest single predictor of student success" (2001, p. 37). Parent–teacher conferencing is one of the most productive ways to achieve this success.

Conferences can be both positive and negative, depending on the teacher's preparation. Poorly conducted conferences can be a waste of time and can even create negative thoughts and feelings between the teacher and the parent. When the teacher makes the best possible use of the conferences and conducts them with skill and understanding, it can be beneficial for all parties. Bulach and Potter (2001) reported several positive ingredients for a successful parent–teacher conference, including the following: 1) being honest about the student's academic performance and behavior, 2) developing an action plan that involves parents, 3) building a relationship of trust and respect, 4) seeking parent input for solutions to problems, and 5) concentrating on the most important concerns by being specific and giving clear examples.

Frontline Perspective

Both in the classroom and in the lofty tower of school administration, whenever I [Martin Ratcliffe] participated in parent meetings with colleagues and parents, I adopted the attitude that parents were partners and friends and we could work collaboratively to help their children succeed in school. This attitude had served me well as a former school principal, causing my secretary to once quip, "Parents come in to your office mad, but they always leave with a smile on their face." I believe this was largely owing to my outlook regarding parents as friends and partners. Teacher–parent meetings were also productive and cordial, and usually ended with an agreed-upon action plan—and satisfied parents.

Follow-up is another important aspect of the parent–teacher conference. It is a good idea for the teacher to send parents a note thanking them for coming to the conference and reminding them what plan of action was agreed upon at the conference. A telephone call a few weeks after the conference may provide the parent additional information and also be a checkup of the workings of the action plan (Bulach & Potter, 2001).

Making the Parent Connection: The Involvement of Fathers

Many schools are now making strides to involve dads, because the involvement of fathers has been linked to successful achievement. A report from the National Center for Education Statistics (1997) found that the involvement of fathers was important to their children's grades. The report showed that "when fathers get involved in their children's education, the children are more likely to get mostly A's in school" (p.1). Former U.S. Secretary of Education Richard W. Riley wrote, "Dads who stay connected—who showed up—reap the rewards when it comes to good report cards" (National Center for Education Statistics, 1997).

One way to involve fathers is through a program modeled on the "McDad's club." This club began when two fathers persuaded a school's PTA to sponsor a dad's club. The McDad's club has three reasons for existence: to help the teachers in any way they can, get the dads involved in special activities at the school, and bring in special speakers that offer topics for dads. Fathers might come to classrooms and read to the children, or enjoy "Donuts with Dads" or "Lunch with Dads" programs. Children without dads are matched up with surrogate fathers so that children are not left out because of separation, death, or their fathers' working commitments. As Elliot commented, "It's important that children see that their dads are interested in their education as well as their moms. But I have found that without a specific invitation, dads don't usually come to school to participate" (1996, p. 54).

Schools need to become more father friendly. Many dads are reluctant to become involved in the educational process of their children because schools have traditionally been considered to be places for women. Shedlin (2004) estimated that 95% percent of elementary school teachers and almost 60% of elementary school principals are women. Shedlin developed a plan for principals to increase the involvement of fathers in their children's education using the following steps:

1. Articulate and demonstrate that home and school are partners in the education of children by creating specific ways to work together on behalf of students.
2. Make a concerted effort to involve dads during the earliest school years, so that from the beginning they feel welcomed and accustomed to being involved.
3. Arrange school meetings at times that dads are likely to be able to attend, even considering Saturdays as an option. (pp. 24–25)

Making the Parent Connection:
Dual-Parent and Single-Parent Involvement

School programs are met with new challenges today as they seek to involve diverse families: single-parent, blended, multigenerational, foster, and same-sex partners. According to Ray, "the majority of today's children—69 percent—live with two married parents, while 23 percent live with a single mother, 5 percent live with a single father, and 4 percent have neither parent present" (2005, p. 73). However, when thinking of the families schools try to reach, it can be helpful to consider the U.S. Census Bureau's (2004) broad definition of *family*: "a group of two people or more related by birth, marriage, or adoption and residing together." It is important to reach out to all families.

Parents who are in the middle of traumatic events in their lives, such as recent separation, divorce, incarceration, or death of a close relative, may not be capable of helping their children while they are seeking help for their own personal situations. Educators need to be understanding of that and make every effort to continue to communicate for the student's sake.

Students Win When Parents and Teachers Collaborate

If teachers can develop relationships with the parents of their students and connect with them as their allies, the children of those parents have a greater chance of success. Teachers will see success in many different areas: academics, deportment, social behavior, community service, and positive attitudes.

All children should have equal opportunity for success regardless of their gender or ethnic group. Parents, teachers, school, and community members need to work together to influence the positive learning of students. With the improvement of parental involvement, the academic and social areas of all students should improve (Feuerstein, 2000).

CASE STUDY
SCHOOL 1

Dave Dannemiller, former principal of Pine Grove Elementary, said that parental support is critical to a school making AYP. "When the parent buys in, there is an attitude that permeates through the whole building," he said. "This was one of those gems that I had no idea had as much of an impact on the progress that Pine Grove made and that was parental involvement and school culture." Among the ways he bolstered parental support was to invite parents to school functions and meetings. He also ensured that parents understood what school improvements were being made and made parents feel they were an integral part of the school improvement process. He explained, "There's that piece of the parental involvement and the involvement of the community in a leadership role, and I embrace that—and parents seem to be aware of the fact that they did have a say and that they did have some control as to what direction the school was going and they appreciated being heard."

Dannemiller even instituted a requirement for 9 parent volunteer hours per year. Parents could volunteer to participate in parent workshops that teachers were required to offer on ways to help children academically at home, or parents could serve on various committees and school and parent organizations. In exchange, the parents who completed 9 hours would have the option of selecting their child's teacher for the next school year, and their child would receive a school shirt similar to the staff shirts. Those who did not complete their volunteer hours did not have that option. Dannemiller said that he capped parent choice for the classes at only one third, and the other two thirds were school selected to ensure heterogeneous grouping. He said, "I know a lot of my colleagues don't buy into parents selecting teachers and [they believe] that shouldn't be happening because it becomes a popularity contest. But I came at it from the point of view that I would be hypocritical if I say that I want you to be involved in your child's education, but I don't want to hear what teacher you want for your child."

Dannemiller said he saw his parent volunteer hours increase. He said teacher choice was on a first-come, first-served basis, and parents came in on a selected day to put in their requests. "It was like people lined up for concert tickets," he said. "They even had lounge chairs and coffee." Based on Lezotte's and McKee's (2002) definition, Pine Grove Elementary is an *advanced* effective school, because a community of parents and teachers work together to move students forward academically. The relationships between the parents and teachers are strong, because under the principal's leadership and direction they must work together to increase student achievement. There is a strong expectation that parents will participate and be included in schoolwide decisions that will affect the growth and development of their child.

CASE STUDY
SCHOOL 2

John D. Floyd K-8 Environmental Science School, on the other hand, did not have parent involvement as strong as Pine Grove's, which is part of why it can be considered a *proficient* school rather than advanced. Parents were visible throughout the school as volunteers. They worked in the cafeteria, assisted in the front office, and some substituted for teachers who may have had to leave early for the day. There were fundraisers, parent meetings, and field trips. However, the former principal, Dr. Marcia Austin, admits that parent outreach could have been much stronger. Although there were the PTA and the School Advisory Council, there was room for much more parent involvement, and parents could have received more invitations for greater participation in their child's school. Austin says, "This is an area that I wish we could have done more. However, multiple means of communication is the key. Teachers made at least one phone call to every parent at the beginning of the school year. We strived to maintain an updated web site, access to online grades, newsletters, friendly reception staff, online messaging system, and timely communication about student progress or non-progress." John D. Floyd did not allow parents to choose their child's teacher; Austin explained that she did not want to encourage an environment where certain teachers were favored over others.

The leaping conclusion from comparing Pine Grove with John D. Floyd in the correlate area of Positive Home–School Relations is that the strength of parent involvement played a significant role in Pine Grove's success in making AYP. Both principals believe that parent involvement is a strong component needed in an effective school. However, at Pine Grove parents were required to volunteer and teachers required to offer parent academic workshops. The school also offered parents an opportunity to volunteer for the parent academic workshops. As Pine Grove made AYP consecutively and John D. Floyd did not, it is reasonable to surmise that its strong parental involvement was a contributing factor to students making learning gains.

Frontline Perspective

Until we can go outside of our boundaries and go to where our parents are, we won't meet AYP.

—Middle school assistant principal

SUMMARY

The research as well as personal experience both inform us of the overwhelmingly positive effect parents can (and should) have on the education of their children. The research, including one author's study (Ratcliffe, 2006), clearly shows Positive Home–School Relations to be the number one predictor of student academic achievement, including AYP scores. In addition, former U.S. Secretary of Education Riley (1994) reminded us that families are the foundation on which a strong education is built. Armed with this knowledge, it behooves all educators to build bridges from where the parents are to where the school is. We must serve parents by building opportunities where they can be actively involved in the lives of their children. This is not an easy task, but it can and must happen if we are to see our students really excel at school. Implementing the strategies outlined in this chapter will assist educators with the momentous task of increasing student achievement and helping schools to make the grade.

CHAPTER REFLECTION

1. Discuss your response to the chapter prompt by former U.S. Secretary of Education Richard W. Riley: "The American family is the rock on which a solid education can and must be built" (1994, para. 4). Do you agree/disagree with this statement? Explain. How can schools create a forum that fosters a positive partnership with parents? Explain your response and give specific examples.

2. Summarize what the research says about the importance of positive home–school relations. Identify two or three capstone studies that reinforce the importance of this correlate.

3. Compare and contrast the strategies used by the two case study schools. Which strategies contributed to one school making AYP and the other failing to make AYP?

4. List the top five correlate strategies that you could implement to boost the presence of this correlate in your school district, school, or classroom. Why did you choose them? How would you implement them? How would you assess their effectiveness?

5. How important is the involvement of fathers in their children's education? Explain. What top three strategies could you implement to increase the positive involvement of fathers in the education of their children? Give examples of how you would implement these strategies.

6. Give a scenario of how you have used (or could use) the strategies listed in the parent conference section successfully. What was (or could be) the outcome of the conference?

Opportunity to Learn and Student Time on Task Correlate

with Mary Brezinski and Glenn S. Gardner

Given sufficient time (and appropriate types of help), 95 percent of students (the top 5 percent + the next 90 percent) can learn a subject up to a high level of mastery.

—S.B. Bloom (1968, p. 4)

Correlate Definition   In the effective school, teachers allocate a significant amount of classroom time to instruction in the essential curricular areas. For a high percentage of this time, students are actively engaged in whole-class or large-group, teacher-directed, planned, learning activities. (Lezotte & McKee, 2002, p. 19)

Once when I [Martin Ratcliffe] was a school principal and teacher concurrently at a small school, new students were included because of rezoning changes. These students had previously not had the opportunity to attend an advanced school. Initially, large amounts of teacher-directed instructional time were spent on essential skills, enabling each student to reach first-generation proficiency. However, as the year progressed, increased amounts of time were spent using advanced instructional strategies such as interdisciplinary learning. Students were constantly immersed in engaging learning opportunities and challenged to reach advanced academic levels. As teachers, we practiced organized abandonment of less important curriculum content. The exposure to in-depth learning paid off. Each of the integrated students excelled academically. Indeed, several were awarded the student-of-the-year prize for outstanding academic achievement.

IMPORTANCE OF OPPORTUNITY TO LEARN AND STUDENT TIME ON TASK

Understandably, with or without interruptions, keeping students engaged and motivated to learn in the time given can be daily challenges for the classroom teacher. Marzano (2007) states, "Although it is probably not the job of classroom teachers to entertain students, it is the job of every classroom teacher to engage students. One might argue that this is becoming increasingly more difficult in a society of fast-paced media and video games" (p. 98). For the purpose of this book, *time on task* means students are engaged in the instructional activity during a given period of time. As Blackburn aptly states,

> In brief, it really boils down to what degree students are involved in and participating in the learning process. So, if I'm actively listening to a discussion, possibly writing down things to help me remember key points, I'm engaged. But if I'm really thinking about the latest video game and I'm nodding so you think I'm paying attention, then I'm not. It's that simple." (2005, p. 28)

It may be simple to notice that students are *off* task, but teachers struggle with keeping students *on* task on any given day during the school year. One day there may be a bird at the window that is more intriguing than estimating the place value to the nearest hundredth, or another day a student's new pencil case with Zac Efron's tiny face etched in may compete with the definition of a verb. No one said it was easy, but to keep students on task teachers must focus on utilizing several different types of strategies. Some of these strategies are outlined in Marzano's book, *The Art and Science of Teaching* (2007). Here are a few other practical strategies shared by teachers in our online survey:

Frontline Perspective

As a district math coach, I have a variety of trainings, but my main emphasis to teachers is to use time wisely and effectively during their instruction. They must involve students in the lesson. I encourage them to have cooperative groups such as think/pair/share activities.

—District math coach

1. Use an online timer and project it on your overhead.
2. Use manipulatives.
3. Differentiate your instruction.
4. Keep the lesson exciting and moving along (animation or props are always helpful).
5. Begin lessons with a question and allow students to share background knowledge. You will get buy-in to the lesson.
6. Nurture curiosity. Bring in or show something unusual to jump-start the discussion for the lesson.

7. Use high-interest Internet sites (e.g., Brainpop, United Streaming).

8. Call on students at random.

9. Use Active Boards (electronic whiteboards) and student response systems to create a gaming-like feel to your lesson.

10. During discussions, solicit volunteers or call on those suspected of being off task.

Blackburn (2005) sums it up in a play on the title of Robert Fulgham's *All I Really Need to Know I Learned in Kindergarten* (2004). She lists five clear concepts she calls "All I Ever Needed to Know About Student Engagement I Learned Watching a Kindergarten Teacher":

> (1) Make it fun, and learning happens; (2) Build routines, and everyone knows what to expect; (3) Keep students involved, and they stay out of trouble; (4) Make it real, and students are interested; (5) Work together, and everyone accomplishes more. (p. 29)

No matter which strategies are chosen, the fact is that teachers must find a way to keep all students on task. Of course, it is impractical to say that can happen all the time. However, with a focus on the correlate Opportunity to Learn and Student Time on Task, teachers have won half the battle in keeping students engaged in the instruction, and thus student learning and achievement can increase.

STRATEGIES FOR IMPROVING OPPORTUNITY TO LEARN AND INCREASING STUDENT TIME ON TASK

There are several core tasks that underlie strategies for improving students' opportunity to learn and time on task: development, survey use, prioritizing, strategizing, program creation, learning, management, planning, engagement, and assessment. These considerations are important at every level.

What Highly Effective Superintendents and District Administrators Do

The following are *development* strategies that highly effective superintendents and district administrators use to broadly support improved student opportunity to learn.

- Provide district in-service trainings on cooperative learning and differentiated learning strategies for all curriculum specialists, resource teachers, and classroom teachers.

- Support the mentoring program by providing resources for teacher mentors to use in order to model techniques to increase student engagement in the classroom.
- Collaborate with district technology specialists to integrate technology effectively into the curriculum.
- Require administrators' professional development plans to contain strategies on how they will increase learning opportunities in their school.

Also at the district level, *surveys* can be conducted to inform district leaders about what broader initiatives should be taken.

- Administer a correlate survey to get a baseline for all the correlates, including the Opportunity to Learn and Time on Task correlate (e.g., Cardella & Sudlow, 2000; Effective Schools, n.d.).
- Utilize the correlate survey results in a stepwise statistical regression analysis to identify districtwide student achievement predictor correlates.

Frontline Perspective

I guide teachers in analyzing data to make instructional decisions in the classroom and provide research-based and evidence-based professional development so that teachers can maximize their instruction.

—Academic intervention facilitator

What Highly Effective
Principals and School Administrators Do

Principals and school-level administrators foster student opportunities to learn by *prioritizing:*

- Realign the school mission with that of the district, state, and federal government.
- Practice active, systematic, and ongoing deselection of items that do not align with the "new" school vision and mission.
- Highly effective principals and school-level administrators also *strategize* to ensure that maximum time on task is possible.
- Plan the master schedule with the focus on keeping classroom instruction sacred.
- Require advance notification for any changes to the master schedule.

Frontline Perspective

We provide opportunities for teachers to use data to drive instruction. We guard instructional time through designating "non-interruption" days.

—Assistant principal of curriculum

- Plan meetings strategically, allowing teachers to optimize their planning times.
- Require procedures and protocols for announcements and phone calls to classrooms.

Finally, highly effective principals and school administrators *create programs* to help their teachers make the most of students' learning time.

- Provide time for professional learning communities to learn about "on time, on task" and student engagement strategies.

Frontline Perspective

I constantly evaluate student data from periodic assessments and grades. I speak with teachers so that they can fine tune their lessons to meet the needs of the students. I also monitor teaching on a regular basis through classroom observations and give teachers the needed feedback to improve their lessons.

—Middle school principal

- Create a teacher mentor program to pair new (and less effective) teachers with experienced teachers who model these correlate strategies.

What Highly Effective Teachers Do

Highly effective classroom teachers focus on *learning*, employing research-based and evidence-based learning strategies, including cooperative learning and directed instruction.

They also take care in their *management* strategy to do the following:

- Adhere to and (daily) reinforce clear procedures and protocols.
- Teach, model, and guide students bell to bell, and provide ample learning time in class—no wasted time.
- Use strong classroom management.

Additional strategies teachers can use for *planning* are

- Prepare well
- Know their content or subject well
- Adjust their plans regularly based on feedback from state, district, school, and classroom data

Effective teachers also use the following strategies to *engage* their students. Specific examples of how these look in action are shown in Tables 4.1 and 4.2.

- Arouse students' curiosity by asking essential higher-order critical thinking and problem-solving questions.

Table 4.1.   Key strategies teachers can use to engage students and maximize the opportunity for learning

Strategy	Definition	Example: Thematic unit on slavery
Shoulder partners or face partners	For discussion purposes (Kagan & Kagan, 2008). Shoulder partner: Partner next to student. Face partner: Partner across from student.	Introduce students to a thematic unit on slavery. Students look at a book cover on a book about slavery (*Molly Bannaky*; McGill, 1999) and make predictions about the content of the book. They share these predictions with their shoulder partner or face partner. Then they share their predictions with the cooperative group to see if there are different predictions.
Think alouds or say somethings	A "think aloud" allows the student to slow the reading process down and construct meaning from the text. In the "say something" reading strategy, a student collaborates with a partner and then responds to what has been read.	After introducing the text, start reading the text, stopping periodically to have students think aloud with their shoulder/face partners. The during-reading strategy of "say something often" can also be used (Beers, 2003). Say something often starters include "I predict that . . . " "Because this happened [fill in detail], then I think this [fill in detail] is going to happen." "I wonder if . . . " "What would happen if . . . " "Who is . . . " "Do you think that . . . " "At first I thought [fill in detail], but now I think [fill in detail]." "This part is really saying . . . " "This is good because . . . " "This is hard because . . . " "This is confusing because . . . " "My favorite part so far is . . . " "This reminds me of . . . " "This character [fill in name] is like [fill in name or thing] because . . . " "This setting reminds me of . . . "
Activation of prior knowledge	Comprehension is enhanced when students have prior knowledge of a subject area.	Students do a brainstorming free-writing activity on the subject of slavery. If students first write about a topic, they are more likely to want to read about it (Elbow, 2004). After they write for 1–2 minutes, students share what they already know about the subject with their partners and then their cooperative learning group.

Table 4.1. *(continued)*

Strategy	Definition	Example: Thematic unit on slavery
Anticipation guide	An "anticipation guide" is a set of generalizations related to a theme.	Anticipation guides are used to activate engagement in learning. For example, students must check "agree" or "disagree" for the following statements: 1) The age of 17 is too young for a girl to be on her own; 2) It is morally wrong to grow tobacco; 3) No one should have owned slaves in colonial times; 4) We should always comply with the law.
		In order to fill out this anticipation guide, students must discuss the sentences and come to consensus within their cooperative learning group (Beers, 2003).
What if . . . ?	Post-reading strategy that revisits the anticipation guide and asks "what if?" questions. It takes important elements of the text and changes them. Students must discuss how the story would change based on their "what if?"	When the read-aloud comes to an end, have students process what they heard by talking with their cooperative group. Possible "what if" questions related to the unit on slavery include the following related to *Molly Bannaky*: What if Molly did not know how to read? How would history in America have changed? What if Molly had not purchased a slave? What if Molly and Bannaky had four sons instead of four daughters? What if Molly had died instead of Bannaky? What if Molly and Bannaky were jailed for breaking colonial law when they married?

Note: This table is based on contributions by Janet Deck, Ed.D., Assistant Professor of Reading Education, Southeastern University; used by permission.

- Use engaging strategies such as "shoulder or face partners," "think alouds or say somethings," and "what ifs" (see Table 4.1).
- Scaffold instruction to meet the needs of all students—model the task, then guided practice, small group, and independent practice.
- Use cooperative learning and projects to engage students in in-depth learning.
- Use props, models, visual aids, and technology effectively.

Finally, *assessment* is a critical component for ensuring that students have the opportunity to learn. Highly effective teachers

- Include a monitoring system to see that students are learning

Frontline Perspective

Change things around often; start out the lesson with an activity that engages the students. I also circulate the room—never remaining in one place.

—Elementary school teacher

Table 4.2.   Key strategies that highly effective teachers of all students, including English language learners, can use to engage students in learning and enhance academic achievement

Strategy	Definition	Example
Inclusion model	English language learners (ELLs) are included in general education classes.	K–12 teachers are required to teach the same grade-level appropriate content lessons to the English speakers and ELLs. Teachers must be knowledgeable in theories of second language acquisition as well as grade-level content information.
Comprehensible content	Teachers instruct language learning students one level higher than the student's current linguistic skill level (Diaz-Rico & Weed, 2005).	Instructors must be able to distinguish between a student's interpersonal language capabilities and academic functions in order to determine how to most effectively deliver instruction. Interpersonal language is conversational in nature and academic language is scholarly. Therefore, teachers must learn how to make the language of content lessons comprehensible, in both interpersonal and academic ways, to language learners in order to boost achievement for ELLs (Cummins, 2006).
Cooperative learning	Student teams are used to instruct students.	Cooperative learning works for ELLs, because allowing students to work in teams allows for more language practice with peers. ELLs feel more comfortable speaking with their peers. ELLs learn content and language while working with peers (Kagan, 2002).
Scaffolding	Instruction builds on what students know. This is based on the work of Vygotsky, who proposed that with an adult's assistance, children should accomplish tasks that they ordinarily could not perform independently (Larkin, 2002).	The goal of any teacher is to help students learn to accomplish tasks independently. 1. The teacher models the task. 2. The class practices as a whole group with the teacher. 3. The class practices without the teacher. 4. The individual students practice independently (Larkin, 2002). With modeling first, the students see and hear how the task should be completed. This gives students the background knowledge necessary for success on the task once they begin to work individually.

Note: This table is based on contributions by Amy N. Bratten, M.A., TESOL, Assistant Professor of ESOL and Education, Southeastern University; used by permission.

- Ensure that formal and informal assessments are directly tied to instruction
- Utilize criterion-based reference testing regularly

Supportive Research

The advent of NCLB has resulted in teachers and students being under the mallet to produce acceptable AYP scores for all subgroups of the school population or face dire consequences. Schools are rethinking their use of time and how to engage students meaningfully in learning. Students who are targeted as requiring remediation may be pulled from specials (i.e., art, music, physical education) or required to attend remediation classes before or after school. This requires time and strategic planning, yet when school schedules maximize time available for learning and provide engaging and well-structured lessons that target key instructional content, students can truly be expected to learn (WestEd Policy Brief, 2001).

Allocated Time and Academic Learning

Academic learning time is a fraction of allocated time in any school subject, but it is the most important factor related to learning. Doubling the amount of learning time does not necessarily double the amount of academic achievement. However, a smaller increase in time can improve student success if the time is used well (Rangel, 2007).

With the pressure to produce tangible AYP results, teachers may be tempted to speed up the curriculum but not cover it in any depth. Donderlinger (1986) reminds us that "education means developing the mind not stuffing the memory" (p. 16). In one study, different students were taught the same content by the same teacher using increasingly streamlined versions of the curriculum. Results showed that as the curriculum was streamlined, students' performance on written questions that assessed their conceptual understanding declined, although they still performed well on the multiple-choice questions. These results demonstrate how reduced time may allow content to be covered but not deeply learned (Clark & Linn, 2003).

The preponderance of research indicates that allocating more time is only part of the solution to enhancing student learning. Other factors such as class size and attendance also affect student achievement. However, using time well is crucial to student achievement.

Length of Day and School Year

For the past 150 years, American public schools have held time constant, while learning has been variable. The average school year lasts 9 months, offers a six-period day with about 5.6 hours of instructional time, and averages 51 minutes per class. The philosophy is simple: learn what you can in the time made available (National Education Commission on Time and Learning, 1994).

Research has shown that the average child in the United States spends two thirds of his or her waking hours in a nonschool environment and only 183 out of 365 days a year in school (Hofferth & Sandberg, 2001). Extensive research has found that as much as 20%–25% of the school day is spent in noninstructional activities such as lunch, recess, trips to the bathroom, and so forth. For example, Caldwell, Huitt, and Graeber (1982) compiled data to demonstrate how academic learning time in the average elementary classroom is less than 1 hour per day. They hold that more efficient use of classroom time by the teacher will increase student academic achievement. Huitt (2006) reiterated the need for increased academic learning time in classrooms. He asserts that small increases in the following factors will result in increased academic learning time and therefore increased student academic achievement: school year length, attendance for year, school day length, allocated time, instructional time, and engaged time. A study looking at K–12 mathematics and science effectiveness inside the classroom also stresses the need for more efficient use of classroom time. Researchers Weiss, Pasley, Smith, Banilower, and Heck (2003) found that "the weakest elements of lesson design are the adequacy of time and structure provided for sense-making, and the adequacy of time and structure provided for lesson wrap-up" (p. x).

Perie, Griggs, and Donahue (2005) suggest that 300 minutes a day for the instructional program should be nested within a school day that is between 360 and 400 minutes long. What does this mean to classroom teachers? It means that students spend significant amounts of time in school, and teachers need to ensure that students are meaningfully engaged in learning for the maximum amount of time possible.

Innovative programs are starting to experiment with different ways to improve student achievement. The Knowledge Is Power Program (KIPP), a national network of college-preparatory public schools for children from underserved communities, has lengthened its school day, added 4 hours every other Saturday, and added 3 weeks in the summer (Education Policy Institute, 2005). Rangel noted, "Nationwide, some schools have changed their start times to 9 a.m. This enables them to conduct intervention sessions from 8:00 a.m. to 8:50 a.m. before school for students who need extra help" (2007, p. 3). Farbman and Kaplan (2005) support the idea of increasing students' learning time. They suggest that contemporary students are expected to do and know more than their predecessors, yet the traditional 180 day school year calendar remains unchanged. They use the analogy of expecting a runner to run a 10-kilometer race in the same time as they completed the 5-kilometer race. They stress that the issue of more school time has largely been overlooked in school reform. In Massachusetts, a statewide initiative has offered funds to add 90–120 minutes to daily schedules, with more time for math, reading, science, electives, and recess (Farbman & Kaplan). The idea seems to be that more school time may be needed by some students to master the challenging state standards.

After-School Programs

After-school programs afford another potential opportunity to engage students in meaningful academic learning, but the research appears to be a mixed bag. A 2003 study by the U.S. Department of Education found that the after-school program initiated by the 21st Century Community Learning Centers showed limited academic impact on reading test scores and grades in most subjects for students who participated in the program (U.S. Department of Education, 2003). A 2008 study of the enhanced academic instruction in after-school programs revealed similar results on the program's impact on reading scores as measured by SAT 10 reading test scores. However, the math portion of the program showed a significant increase on math scores as measured by the SAT 10 math test (Redbeck Black, Doolittle, Zhu, Unterman, & Baldwin Grossman, 2008).

Researchers, looking at 35 after-school programs across the country that they considered top-notch, reached similar conclusions. They found that disadvantaged students who regularly attended those programs for 2 or more years were able to make greater gains in math than did their peers who spent more out-of-school time in unsupervised activities. However, gains in reading were stagnant (Viadero, 2008).

Extended School Year

Studies show that disadvantaged students in elementary school fall behind dramatically over the summer months. By the time students reach ninth grade, two thirds of the achievement gap between disadvantaged and advantaged students is directly related to the so-called "summer learning loss." Some educational policy makers see year-round schooling as a way of making up for all that lost time, but few studies have found it to be an effective strategy. The reason is that most year-round schedules rearrange instructional time rather than extend it (Viadero, 2008). However, van der Graaf (2008) found a statistically significant relationship between the extended school year and student academic achievement. Similarly, a supportive study by the NGA Center for Best Practices (2009) found that expanded learning opportunities (which include after-school, summer learning, and extended day and extended year programs) can help states reduce dropout rates and increase graduation rates. The study stresses that governors must couple reform-based attempts with increased availability of high-quality expanded learning opportunities, especially for the at-risk population, noting that "students who are at risk of dropping out may need more than a typical school day to succeed" (p. 8).

Summer School and Saturday School

According to a study by Cooper, Charlton, Valentine, and Muhlenbruck (2000), summer learning programs gave students a healthy learning boost. These programs were designed to tutor failing or at-risk students, enrich children's lives, or step up the pace of learning. The most effective summer school programs are the ones that incorporate the so-called best practice principles; what counts is how the extra learning time is used. Many charter schools and Title I schools implement summer programs and occasional Saturday classes to help prepare students to succeed in school.

SUMMARY

The NCLB Act of 2001 mandates that schools will be held accountable for 100% proficiency of AYP for all students. Undeniably, the quality of time and the quantity of time allocated to learning will help educators to achieve this goal. Although increasing the amount of time on task is a key factor to student achievement, by itself it has little direct impact. The key variable to making instructional time effective is left in the hands of educators. Educators need to match mastery skills with student ability and learning styles in order to make effective use of time. The amount of time in which students are actively and appropriately engaged in learning will determine the amount of success each student will achieve. This is true of all students and is especially true for the growing population of English speakers of other languages, who are a targeted subgroup under NCLB. They must show substantial learning gains in order for a school to make AYP.

Schools must cultivate a business and purposeful type of efficiency that maximizes student learning time and drastically reduces classroom interruptions. That is, schools should operate in a professional, business-like manner, making full use of classroom time and keeping the focus on student learning. Teacher contact with students should be strategic and purposeful. Teachers should be armed with a pedagogical arsenal that they can strategically employ to effect maximum learning for all students, including English language learners. In addition to being pedagogical clinicians, teachers must be content-proficient, master classroom managers, competent interdisciplinary practitioners, knowledgeable in data-driven instructional practices, knowledgeable in theory and practice of teaching to speakers of other languages, and expert time strategists who maximize opportunities for student learning and student time on task—for all students. Remember, "Given sufficient time (and appropriate types of help), 95 percent of students (the top 5 percent + the next 90 percent) can learn a subject up to a high level of mastery" (Bloom, 1968, p. 4). There is no time to waste for educators who operationalize this correlate, as it helps schools to make the grade.

CASE STUDIES
SCHOOLS 1 AND 2

There is nothing exciting or distinctive about school schedules and routines. Both Pine Grove and John D. Floyd K-8 Environmental Science schools adhere to a schedule that honors the Opportunity to Learn and Student Time on Task Correlate, both schools have routines, and both schools have a culture that knows the time pressure on an instructional day that is measured by minutes and a well-paced curriculum guide. It is within this structured schedule that teachers must ensure that students are focused and on task, that instructional strategies are effective and consistent, and that measureable learning outcomes are achieved in every subject.

Administrators at both schools ensure that there is an opportunity to learn because instructional time is protected from interruptions by 1) creating a master calendar that does not interfere with instruction, 2) monitoring all announcements made on the intercom, and 3) limiting the number of teacher meetings and classroom visits. Principal Dannemiller of Pine Grove and Principal Austin of John D. Floyd said that the master calendar is created before the beginning of the school year, with school assemblies and events scheduled at a minimum. At both schools, any changes to the master calendar are made in advance with the understanding that instructional time is sacred, especially in the core academic subject areas.

In addition, both administrators emphasized that all announcements had to be cleared through them when they were principals at their respective schools, and they stressed that intercom and phone interruptions were kept to a minimum. Teacher meetings and classroom visits were also monitored and scheduled at both schools. Dannemiller said, "Since we expected the teachers to do quality lesson plans, then we had to watch how we structured meetings, especially during the teachers' planning time. Meetings had to be scheduled at least 2 weeks in advance. We also let parents know that goodies for parties could only be done at the end of the day before dismissal."

Both schools included a 90-minute, mandatory reading block with an emphasis on guided reading and small-group instruction. This time was not interrupted, as Dannemiller stated: "We posted our reading block times on the doors so that they [teachers and students] were not to be disturbed." Math was another core subject for which both schools allocated uninterrupted time; each scheduled at least 60 minutes for a math block.

Austin said she also created opportunities for extended learning time by temporarily suspending electives and offering after-school instruction in math, reading, and writing. "There's just not enough time in the day to teach and allow for learning. So, as a principal, I had to be creative and give students more time and learning experiences at the end of the day," she said, emphasizing that she could not have done it without the teachers' support and parental approval.

For the Opportunity to Learn and Student Time on Task correlate, Pine Grove Elementary is advanced compared with John D. Floyd, which is proficient. This is based on a decline in John D. Floyd's Effective School Survey Correlate (Effective Schools, n.d.) data comparison from 2006 to 2008. The decline in this correlate shows that teachers believed that they did not have enough time to dedicate to student learning and effective classroom instruction. The increase in the number of classroom intercom interruptions and student pull-outs for testing and discipline were cited as reasons for the decline. Pine Grove, comparatively, was able to effectively control the number of intercom and student disruptions to the classroom environment. In addition, the requirement that Pine Grove's teachers and administrators schedule meetings 2 weeks in advance allowed for stability and predictability in the schedule. This created an environment where student instructional time was maximized.

CHAPTER REFLECTION

1. Do you agree or disagree with the chapter prompt that sufficient time and the right interventions will allow most students to achieve mastery of the learning material? Explain your response, and give specific examples.

2. Give examples of strategies you would use to enable English language learners to master curriculum content. Explain how you would implement these strategies and why.

3. Compare and contrast the strategies used by the two case study schools. Which strategies would you identify as proficient and advanced? Explain.

4. Identify the correlate strategies you would use to introduce students to a new thematic unit of your choice. Explain how you would actively engage learners using these strategies.

5. List the top three to five correlate strategies that you could implement to boost the presence of this correlate in your school district, school,

or classroom. Why did you choose them? How would you implement them? How would you assess their effectiveness?

6. Summarize the research study you find to be most supportive of the correlate Opportunity to Learn and Student Time on Task. How does this study enhance the correlate?

7. What is your favorite frontline strategy? How would you use this strategy to boost the chapter correlate?

Climate of High Expectations Correlate

with Helene Robinson

All things are possible to him who believes. (Mark 9:23, NKJV)[1]

You can do it if you believe you can!

—Napoleon Hill (1928, p. 18)

Correlate Definition   In the effective school, there is a climate of high expectations in which the staff believes and demonstrates that all students can obtain mastery of the school's essential curriculum. They also believe that they, the staff, have the capability to help all students obtain that mastery. (Lezotte & McKee, 2002, p. 18)

From my [Helene Robinson's] personal experience teaching high school students with autism who lacked basic reading skills of blending, segmenting, and letter-sound correspondence, I found that any age student could learn these skills even though others had deemed them as incapable of learning to read. I was determined to prove to everyone that these young men could learn to read! I knew that I had the skills, the training, and the experience to accomplish this. I had excellent behavior management skills due to graduate studies and 9 years of teaching students with behavior disorders, and had recently completed all the course work for adding reading endorsement to my professional certificate. I felt confident in the pedagogy of teaching reading and managing disruptive behavior. My self-efficacy was high! I believed that I had the power to produce that effect. None of these students had even basic phonemic awareness skills when I received them, and after a few years of my instruction some of them were reading and comprehending at a fourth-grade level. What made the difference? Why were they now learning and had

---

[1]Scripture taken from the New King James Version®. Copyright © 1982 by Thomas Nelson, Inc. Used by permission. All rights reserved.

never mastered this earlier in the first 8 years of their public education? Was it really just that I had high expectations for them? Did my high self-efficacy influence my students' achievements? What are the school factors, teacher factors, and district factors that will create an environment of high expectations for all students, especially for our students with disabilities? This chapter focuses on the Climate of High Expectations correlate.

IMPORTANCE OF ESTABLISHING A CLIMATE OF HIGH EXPECTATIONS

Proficient schools create a climate of high expectations and boast a staff that believe they have the capability of enabling all students to master the essential curriculum. However, advanced schools put their beliefs into practice by ensuring that all students acquire mastery of the essential curriculum. They go beyond just the high expectations to implementing the necessary strategies to ensure learning success for each student.

Setting high standards is inherent in the NCLB mandate. Schools must show overall learning gains and learning gains within each of the student subgroups such as Native American/Alaskan Native, Asian/Pacific Islander, Black, Hispanic, White, Limited English Proficiency, Economically Disadvantaged, and Students with Disabilities (Illinois State Board of Education, n.d.).

Expectations have to be set for each of these subgroups so that schools can show a year's worth of growth. These expectations, then, have to be transferred into measurable student goals, and those students have to understand how to accomplish these goals. Moreover, those students have to *believe* that they can accomplish these goals and meet the expectations to show learning gains in that subject area. This belief in self can be more difficult for struggling students who have faced disappointments in their grades and thus lack confidence in their ability to succeed. But, as Crew (2007) says, a teacher's expectations can make a difference in whether that child attempts to succeed or willingly fails:

Frontline Perspective

Through hard work, discovery, and fun, we work all year for each of us to continue to reach our fullest potential.

—Elementary school teacher

Expectations make or break a student's experience. They show love and faith and belief that a child can do great things; they are an expression of caring, and without them caring can become pity. High expectations are critical because they deal with one's self in the moment, and learning is all about being in a moment where the task is *yours*, the victory is *yours*, the feat is *yours*, the effort is *yours*. You have to *want* to become smarter. You have to *want* to get better, and as an aspect of the student-teacher relationship that belief is not just about the kid. It also has everything to do with the teacher, as an adult person in the child's life, believing that there's something within that child that she wants him to go find and bring back to the task at hand so together they can figure out how to crack that nut. (p. 67)

STRATEGIES FOR ESTABLISHING AND MAINTAINING A CLIMATE OF HIGH EXPECTATIONS

As a component of a district's, school's, and classroom's climate, establishing and maintaining high expectations is a task for all members of the education community. At the various levels, strategies for improving a climate of high expectations involve administration, creation of mission statements and relationships, demonstrations, incentives, collaboration, attendance, and practice.

What Highly Effective Education Professionals at All Levels Do

There are several strategies that apply at all levels:

- Develop and communicate a coherent mission that reflects high expectations and is supported by all constituents.
- Foster positive relationships. Send personal, hand-written notes of encouragement and specific praise to your school leaders.
- Demonstrate high expectations in your personal and professional life.
- Provide a quality curriculum by consistently aligning assessment and instructional practices with K–12 curricular standards.

Furthermore, at the school level, both administrators and teachers do the following:

- Create a school atmosphere of problem solving, warmth, playfulness, informality and cheerful camaraderie among the teachers and the students.
- Foster positive relationships and show that they care what happens to others outside of the classroom.
- Demonstrate aim-for-the-heart principles with all constituents, but especially with teachers, staff, and students. (Aim-for-the-heart means genuinely caring about the affective side of people—their thoughts and feelings first. The assumption is if people feel right, they will think right.)

What Highly Effective
Superintendents and District Administrators Do

At the district level, superintendents and district administrators are uniquely positioned to use *administrative* strategies to build the climate of high expectations. They

- Administer a self-efficacy test to all teacher applicants
- Require teachers to take in-service hours in differentiating instruction, positive behavior supports, and reading instruction

Highly effective superintendents and district administrators also develop *incentive* programs. For example, they offer a stipend to attract teachers to become highly qualified and teach in shortage areas and in schools with high percentages of students who are receiving special education services and/or who have low socioeconomic status.

What Highly Effective
Principals and School Administrators Do

At the school level, highly effective principals and administrators *collaborate* to help shape the school's environment using these strategies:

- Pair new and unqualified teachers with highly qualified, effective, and experienced mentor teachers.
- Plan the master schedule so that special education teachers and extracurricular teachers are planning and co-teaching with the general education teachers to facilitate differentiated and inclusive instruction in all content areas.
- Assign students in classes so that the ratio of students with disabilities to students without disabilities equals the ratio represented in the school population.

They can also *demonstrate* the climate of high expectations by visiting classrooms often to monitor the quality of teacher instruction. Finally, principals and school administers support a climate of high expectations by offering incentives to hire highly effective, caring, and qualified teachers.

Frontline Perspective

We require lesson plans to be submitted on a monthly basis. Grade-level meetings are once a week. Unless there is an emergency, faculty meetings are biweekly. Reading Leadership and Data Review meetings are once a month. Secretarial staff, paraprofessionals, and custodians also meet once a month. Bus drivers meet twice a year.

—Middle school assistant principal

What Highly Effective Teachers Do

Teachers often most directly affect the climate experienced by the students. They support high expectations when they *attend* to their own education and

- Take courses in their subject area(s)
- Take training on differentiating instruction, positive behavior supports, and reading instruction

They also have the first-hand responsibility for *creating* the overall climate for students, so important strategies are to

- Create a climate of high expectations for all
- Care outside the classroom, which enables nurturing inside the classroom

Finally, as adults who work most closely with the students, teachers must *demonstrate* and *practice* high expectations. Some strategies they can use to do this follow:

- Go beyond rhetoric and demonstrate through positive attitudes and actions that all students can succeed. (Teachers' attitudes determine students' *altitudes*.)
- Ensure that all students experience success and acquire mastery of the essential curriculum. (Build self-efficacy.)
- Plan collaboratively on a consistent basis to ensure differentiation of instruction for all students.

Frontline Perspective

Teachers need to play an active role in student education by showing students how to achieve, and then modeling that achievement for them. Teachers should encourage the students to answer questions, help each other, study, and complete homework assignments.

—District math coach

Frontline Perspective

At the beginning of the school year, I communicate my expectations and regularly enforce them. During the middle of the school year, I speak individually with each student to discuss their progress as to expectations and academics.

—Middle school teacher

Supportive Research

Research supports the notion that teachers' attitudes influence student learning. For example, Flaherty and Hackler (2010) conducted research to strengthen the intrinsic motivation of fourth- and sixth-grade elementary classrooms in a small midwestern community. Multiple sources of data—including classroom observation checklists, student self-reported surveys, and parent surveys—revealed the problem of low intrinsic motivational behaviors among students. Two intervention strategies were implemented and monitored: differentiated instruction and cooperative learning. The researchers offered "constant reinforcement of realistic, yet high, expectations, along with positive feedback . . . for all students" (p. ii). In addition to improvement in student motivation, students also improved academically.

Brookover and Lezotte (1979) provide another example of the critical impact of teaching personnel on student achievement. They conducted an in-depth analysis of eight elementary schools; six were characterized by improving student achievement and two by declining student achievement. They identified 10 descriptors that differentiated high-achieving and low-achieving schools with similar student compositions. The most prevalent finding concerned teachers' and principals' attitudes toward learning. In declining schools, staff held low opinions of students and their abilities, whereas the obverse was true in improving schools.

Yara (2009) provides a third example of the positive effects of teachers' attitudes on student learning. She conducted a study to find out about the relationship between teachers' attitudes and students' academic achievement in secondary school mathematics. The subjects included 1,542 secondary mathematics students and 123 mathematics teachers. The results showed that teachers had "good and positive attitudes towards the teaching of mathematics" (p. 364). Yara concluded that "teachers' attitude towards the teaching of mathematics plays a significant role in shaping the attitude of students towards the learning of mathematics" (p. 368).

High Expectations and Self-Efficacy

In order to meet high expectations, one must have high self-efficacy. *Self-efficacy* is an individual's belief about their competence on a prospective task. Individuals who enter adulthood poorly equipped with skills and plagued by nagging doubts about their capabilities find adversity in many aspects of their adult life. People need a sense of self-efficacy to apply what they know consistently, persistently, and skillfully, especially when things are not going well and deficient performances carry negative consequences (Bandura, 2001).

Furthermore, this belief of self-efficacy is central among the three modes of human agency (anticipative, purposive, and self-evaluating) and regulates human functioning through cognitive, motivational, affective, and decisional processes (Bandura & Locke, 2003). Self-directed independent learners must develop more than just a set of learning skills—they must develop a self-efficacious attitude, which ultimately leads to thinking independently in society (Eisenberger, Cont-D'Antiono, & Bertrando, 2000). Similarly, perceived self-efficacy is not a measure of the skills one has, but rather a belief about what one can do under different sets of conditions with whatever skills one possesses (Bandura, 1997).

Nicholas (2002) stated that individuals who believe they are capable of successful performance are more likely to choose challenging activities, work hard, and persist when difficulties are encountered. Self-efficacy is believed to have a strong influence on performance, as it affects choice of activities, the amount of effort exercised, and perseverance in the face of difficulty (Bandura, 1997; Eisenberger, Cont-D'Antiono, & Bertrando, 2000; Graham & Harris, 1989). When individuals approach tasks without self-efficacy, they often make poor use of their capabilities. Experiencing success is an integral part of the process of building a strong sense of self-efficacy (Nicholas, 2002).

Romi and Leyser (2006) reported that experience working with students with disabilities was related to general teaching efficacy beliefs, efficacy regarding social relations, and beliefs regarding low achievers but did not affect personal teaching efficacy. *General teaching efficacy* is the belief that the teacher's ability to bring about desired outcomes is limited by factors external to the teacher, such as home environment and family background. *Personal teaching efficacy* is the teacher's belief that he or she has the skills and abilities to influence students' learning and behavior. Tschannen-Moran and Woolfolk-Hoy (2001) showed a relationship between teacher efficacy beliefs and student achievement, motivation, and the student's own sense of self-efficacy. Furthermore, teacher efficacy beliefs were related to the effort they invested in teaching and the goals they set. Teachers with a higher degree of self-efficacy were more open to new ideas and new methods to meet the needs of students, were less critical of student error, and could work longer with struggling students. Emmer and Hickman (1991) and Jordan, Kirkcaly-Iftar, and Diamond (1993) reported that teachers with higher self-efficacy scores were more likely to use positive classroom management strategies. Finally, teachers with a higher sense of self-efficacy were less likely to refer students with learning and behavior problems to special education (Soodak, Podell, & Lehman, 1998).

Frontline Perspective

I expect students to take notes during class, study those notes, and do daily homework.

—*High school English teacher*

Strategies to Improve a Student's Self-Efficacy

As pointed out earlier, struggling students have a lower sense of self-efficacy. What can a teacher do within his or her class to raise the self-efficacy of struggling students? Students obtain self-efficacy information in four ways: enactive mastery (their task performance), vicarious experiences, verbal persuasion, and their physiological reactions or states (Margolis & McCabe, 2006). Based on the information from these four sources, students make a judgment on their ability to succeed on a specific task or related tasks. Teachers can use a variety of strategies to help students recognize the degree to which they succeed on tasks (enactive mastery). These strategies include planning moderately challenging tasks, teaching specific learning strategies, capitalizing on student choice and interest, and reinforcing effort and correct strategy use. In addition, they can provide a variety of vicarious experiences, such as using peer models where students observe others perform a task while listening to an explanation of how peers are doing each step and/or what they are thinking. Verbal persuasion can be used by encouraging students to try; stressing recent success; giving frequent, focused, and task-specific feedback; and stressing functional attribution statements that identify particular causes and affect future behavior. Teachers should use a variety of feedback, including corrective feedback, prompting, process feedback, instructive feedback, and praising (Margolis & McCabe, 2006). Finally, teachers can teach relaxation techniques to help students cope with physiological reactions to a task. By planning strategies around these four sources from which students derive self-efficacy information, teachers can help struggling learners have a greater sense of self-efficacy.

Frontline Perspective

I expect my students to do their very best and succeed. Students are clearly made aware of my expectations as a group and individually.

—Elementary school teacher

Aiming for the Heart

Dr. Samuel Bennett, the 2006 Florida Teacher of the Year, a National Teacher Finalist, and Dean of the College of Education at Southeastern University, Florida, believes child psychologist Dr. Haim G. Ginott's (1965, 2003) assertion that a teacher must capture a child's heart in order for the child to feel right and therefore think right. He adopted the *aim-for-the-heart* philosophy as part of his own classroom management style, as he believes that the best teachers teach from the heart, not just a book. The following brief story by Dr. Bennett illustrates how the application of this philosophy can affect student academic achievement.

Several years ago a young boy entered my fifth-grade classroom for the very first time. He was known to be defiant and apathetic. For the first few weeks it seemed as though he was trying his very best to do his very worst. At first I reacted to his challenging behavior, but after I reviewed his cumulative folder, I realized he had a pattern of negative behavior. I also found out that he was being raised by a single mom and had older siblings. Joseph's father had died when his mother was due to deliver Joseph, just as they were preparing to move to the United States. From that moment onwards, my perspective towards Joseph changed completely. I viewed Joseph as my "mission impossible" and I accepted the mission. I started working more closely with

Joseph and showing an interest in his extracurricular activities as well as his work in the classroom.

The year had its challenges, but Joseph's behavior showed a constant improvement as time progressed. He improved in his academics, too. A few days before the last day of fifth-grade year, we had an award ceremony for all of our fifth graders. I felt as a proud dad as I called Joseph's name for his award for achieving the honor roll during the last 9 weeks, a first for Joseph. Joseph also received a second award from the fifth-grade group as a whole, "The Turnaround Student of the Year." The Scripture tells us in 1 Samuel 16:7 that God does not look at the outward appearance of someone, but rather at their heart. I try to do likewise.

Teacher Quality

Teacher quality is another factor that contributes to a school environment that fosters high expectations. Goldhaber (2003) reviewed various research reports and described five indicators correlated to teacher quality: degree levels, preparation (pedagogical versus subject knowledge), licensure, years of experience, and academic proficiency. In reference to teacher degree levels, Goldhaber states that research does not show a positive correlation between teachers having advanced degrees and student achievement. However, teachers with advanced degrees in specific subjects can have an impact on student learning in those subjects in certain settings. Goldhaber also stated that there is not enough research to make definitive conclusions about the value of state regulation of the teacher market. Commenting on teachers' years of experience, he cites various research and concludes that there is little correlation between years of teaching and student outcomes. Goldhaber defined teachers' general academic proficiency as their intelligence and motivation as measured by performance on tests of verbal ability, teacher licensure, or college entrance exams and by the selectivity of the undergraduate institutions attended by teachers. He cites literature that reports positive relationships between student achievement and teacher academic proficiency and concludes that teacher academic proficiency is one of the best predictors of teacher quality.

Other researchers have found that students taught by teachers holding subject-specific certification achieve more than those who are taught by teachers who do not hold subject-specific certification (Darling-Hammond & Youngs, 2002). In addition, Darling-Hammond and Youngs found that the percentage of teachers with full certification and the percentage of teachers with a subject major predicted higher mathematic and reading achievement. Darling-Hammond (2000) further argues the need for teacher certification by documenting that teachers who do not go through a teacher preparation program have higher attrition rates. This attrition creates a lack of a stable, high-ability teaching force, which further exacerbates the teacher shortage problem. Furthermore, she notes that although it is necessary to have rigorous, professional teaching standards, there is also much variation between states. Such variation creates inequity in students' access to high-quality teaching (Darling-Hammond, 2000), especially in the urban schools (Gehrke, 2005).

Rice (2003) found that subject-specific certification matters in secondary schools but not in elementary schools. In addition, the New York City Board of Education (2000) reported a positive correlation between higher percentages of certified teachers and the percentage of students showing high achievements in reading and math.

Important variables of teacher quality that are not included in the NCLB definition of "highly qualified" are teacher motivation and beliefs. The impact of teacher choice-making and self-efficacy upon observed teacher behaviors is supported by Bandura's (1997) and Glasser's (1998) theories. Kozol (2005) and Noguera (2003) describe the motivation and beliefs of effective urban school teachers, which carry over well to describe effective special education teachers. Kozol (2005) described these effective teachers: "affectionate, confident, morally committed with a fascination and delight with growing children and . . . thoroughly convinced that each and every one of them has an inherent value to begin with" (p. 286). He also stated that successful urban schools produced environments in which effective teaching occurs without the sacrifice of all those elements of warmth, playfulness, informality, and cheerful camaraderie among the teachers and the students. Kozol described an effective small school as one that is "defined not only by its size but also by its sense of mission, as a place indeed that has a sense of mission, with a teaching staff that truly wants to be there in the first place" (p. 275). He further added that students thrive on this sense of warmth and intimacy that the school makes possible. Noguera (2003) notes that in these effective urban schools there is "a quality that produces a high morale and compels those who teach or learn there to work with a sense of purpose and commitment" (p. 21).

Grouping Practices

Teachers should use a flexible approach to grouping so students can get to know all their classmates, to foster a sense that ability is not fixed, and so teachers can target instruction more effectively (Rubin, 2006).

Coelho (1998) stresses the importance of using mixed-ability grouping practices by pointing out the cumulative effects of same-ability grouping practices. Starting in elementary school, students are often grouped by ability within the classroom. Students in low-ability groups do not receive the same quality of instruction and often have unqualified teachers (Coelho, 1998). Elbaum, Vaughn, Hughes, Moody, and Schumm (2000) also found that students in lower ability groups for reading instruction received inferior instruction as measured by instructional time, time on task, meaning orientation to reading tasks, appropriateness of reading materials, and amount of material read. In a cross-national study comparing 46 countries (Akiba, LeTendre, & Scribner, 2007), the opportunity for low socioeconomic status students to be taught by qualified teachers was compared with their high socioeconomic status peers. The resulting difference between the number of high socioeconomic status and low socioeconomic status students taught by qualified teachers was defined as an *opportunity gap.* The higher the opportunity gap, the less opportunity low socioeconomic status students had to be taught by a qualified teacher. The United States opportunity gap was the fourth highest among the 46 countries. There was a 14.4% difference between the number of high socioeconomic status and low socioeconomic status students taught by qualified teachers in the United States, as compared with 21 other countries that had less than a 5% difference. Even when students in low-ability groups have teachers who are committed, enthusiastic, and skilled, it is difficult to establish an effective learning environment in these classrooms because these students recognize and resent their status, respond defensively, and often refuse to participate in the academic efforts that could bring them more success.

Lotan (2006) stresses the need for mixed-ability grouping to create equal-status, balanced interaction among students working in small learning groups. Mixed-ability grouping has several benefits. Burris and Welner (2005) found that students from minority groups participating in mixed-ability classrooms in New York were more likely to graduate with a Regents high school diploma. Another outcome of mixed-ability grouping is that students learn to value working together and appreciate the benefits each can contribute (Lyle, 1999). Boalar (2006) also reported that students increased in their relational equity as well as in their math achievement at an urban, ethnically diverse school that incorporated heterogeneous grouping and complex instruction.

Ansalone (2004) examined results of tracking, including differentiation of the curricula and teacher expectations; school misconduct; race, class, and gender bias; and the development of separate friendship patterns. A key finding is that lower-tracked students sense a differential attitude toward themselves and consequently lower their own expectations (Ansalone, 2004). Belief in personal efficacy diminishes, and students have little incentive to persevere in the face of difficulties (Noguera, 2003).

Professional Development Delivery

In addition to teacher quality factors and the grouping practices of students, the content and delivery of preservice and in-service professional development is another significant factor in creating a school environment of high expectations. Chard (2004) explains that the system variables of professional development are a higher priority than personal variables, as they must exist for individual development. Chard states that system variables such as measurable reading goals, well-designed instructional tools, and teacher support or incentives must be in place in order for professional development to occur. He then proceeds to describe a professional development system that addresses the issues of domain-specific knowledge, general pedagogical knowledge, teachers' capacity to apply their knowledge in the classroom and motivation to improve. Chard claims that the interdependence of these elements of professional development is the key to sustainable reading achievement of students.

Penuel, Fishman, Yamaguchi, and Gallagher (2007), in a study of 454 teachers, examined the effects of different characteristics of professional development on teachers' knowledge and their ability to implement the program they had been trained in at a workshop. They found that incorporating teacher planning time and providing technical support were significant for promoting program implementation. Special education teachers, general education teachers, and extracurricular teachers need to plan collaboratively on a consistent basis so that differentiation of instruction will occur for all students in every classroom.

Professional Development Content

To support the establishment of a climate of high expectations, professional development often needs to be provided in positive behavioral interventions and supports (PBIS), differentiating instruction, and reading instruction (see Table 5.1 for an examination of research findings on professional development in these areas). PBIS, which is based on applied behavior analysis, has been used for years to create individual behavior management plans for students with disabilities with very challenging behavior. It is now used as part of response to intervention initiatives as a schoolwide intervention in many schools across the nation. Clarke and Dunlap (2008) describe PBS as using "data-based accountability, an emphasis on broad outcomes reflecting lifestyle improvements, ecological and social validity, a collaborative approach to planning and implementation, and an emphasis on proactive interventions focusing on instructional and environmental redesign" (p. 69). As previously noted, special education, general education, and extracurricular teachers should plan together regularly to ensure differentiation of instruction for all students in all classrooms. Because 75% to 80% of students in special education with mild disabilities nationwide have significant problems in basic language and reading skills (Pearson, Barr, Mosenthal, & Kamil, 2000), it would seem imperative that teachers of students with disabilities be required to take coursework in the foundations of reading: phonemic awareness, phonics, fluency, vocabulary, and reading comprehension.

Table 5.1. A summary of professional development content and key findings by researchers

Professional development content	Key findings
Positive behavioral interventions and supports (PBIS)	Teachers' collective efficiency on managing student discipline is the single strongest predictor of job satisfaction (Kates & Klassen, 2007).
	Over several years, office referrals and suspensions decreased and student reading and math gains were associated with the implementation of PBIS in urban elementary schools (Luiselli, Putnam, Handler, & Feinberg, 2005).
	There was a reduction of 6,010 office referrals and 1,032 suspensions in 28 early childhood and K–12 schools in New Hampshire. Academic gains in math were associated with implementing PBIS with fidelity (Clarke & Dunlap, 2008).
	High schools using PBIS had improved student behavior, school climate, and improved school completion rates (Bohanon, Flannery, Malloy, & Fenning, 2009).
Differentiated instruction and arts integration	Flexible ability grouping with curricular differentiation brings significant achievement reading gains for average and high ability readers (Tieso, 2003).
	Elementary teachers differentiating instruction increased end-of-year test scores from 79% to 94.8% (Lewis & Batts, 2005).
	Reading levels increase in high school students from 5.9 to 8.2 grade level after 4 years of differentiated instruction (Fisher, Frey, & Williams, 2003).
	Arts integration is particularly important for students with disabilities and students with other learning needs. It develops higher-order language, literacy, writing, and numeracy skills. It enhances perception, memory, and the ability to interpret events and concepts (Mason, Steedly, & Thormann, 2008).
	Students' analytical assessments increased following arts-integrated units but not following traditional units (DeMoss, 2005).
Reading instruction	Benefits of decoding-based reading and intervention program to remediate primary skill deficiencies of all ages with explicit instruction (Endress, Weston, Marchand-Martella, Martella, & Simmons, 2007)
	Teacher attitude and teacher–student collaboration were essential. Strategy instruction is most effective when embedded in contextualized literacy activities. Multifaceted interventions promote more growth (Schmidt, Rozendal, & Greenman, 2002).
	Reading instruction for students with disabilities was most effective in inclusion model with team teaching (Anderson, 2006).
	Review of strategic learning strategies instruction for students with learning disabilities (Nicholas, 2002)
	Tools and activities for secondary English and Exceptional Students in Education teachers (Dieker & Ousley, 2006)
	Interaction between teacher knowledge and decoding instruction; students of more knowledgeable teachers who were exposed to more time with explicit instruction had stronger reading gains. Students of less knowledgeable teachers who were exposed to more time with explicit instruction made weaker reading gains (Piasta, Connor, Fishman, & Morrison, 2009).

SUMMARY

Self-efficacy is at the heart of student academic success. Just like the story "The Little Engine That Could," a student who is expected to succeed and sees himself or herself succeeding is more likely to succeed. The teacher must have high self-efficacy so that he or she can create a high sense of self-efficacy in his or her students. By creating a school environment where the teacher aims for the heart of the child, where instruction is differentiated, positive behavior supports are used, and teachers and administrators really believe in the academic potential of each student, an environment of high expectations can be created and students will rise to the challenge and achieve more. In turn, schools will make the grade!

CASE STUDY
SCHOOL 1

No one is saying that there is a formulaic process or cookie-cutter recipe that educators can rely on to show students how to believe in themselves and reach their goals. However, several effective strategies can help students set high expectations and believe that they can reach them. One was used at Pine Grove Elementary during 2 years the school made AYP (2006–2007 and 2007–2008). The principal at the time, Dave Dannemiller, said that when he first took the leadership reins at the school, he worked on rewriting the school mission and vision statements. The revised vision statement was: "At Pine Grove Elementary, we strive to be our best. We strive to be an empowered, self-motivated community for today and tomorrow." He said that statement set the tone for everything done at the school and laid the foundation for high expectations and student empowerment. He explained,

> The teachers purposely set up situations where the students felt empowered. They had control over their learning and had some self-motivation. So as long as the students were working toward that, then that was okay. Expectations as far as the amount of homework or [where a student should be] at a certain point were not clearly laid out. We focused on laying out expectations to fulfill the mission.

In addition, students had to recite a daily affirmation statement after saying the Pledge of Allegiance. They would simply say, "I am great because I am me. I believe in myself. I feel my best when I do my best." Dannemiller added, "Everything that was presented had a clear focus. If we were introducing this strategy, this program, this approach, then we are going to empower our kids. We even did this when we spoke to the parent and teacher community. We stressed positive reinforcement in everything that we did." He emphasized that he told his teachers that they needed to have high expectations for all students, even those struggling with disabilities. He said, "It makes the hair stand up on the back of my head when classroom teachers make the comment, 'Well that's not my student.' Oh yes he or she is. Yes, he's a student in ESE [Exceptional Student Education], or yes she's an ESOL [English as a Second Language] student, but he or she is also your student. I stressed that we are all accountable for that child."

CASE STUDY
SCHOOL 2

Meanwhile, John D. Floyd Environmental Science K-8 School was in the process of refining its curriculum pacing guides, hiring new teachers, and moving classes as new students enrolled, as the school experienced significant growth going into the 2007–2008 school year. Still, then-principal Marcia Austin said, "Most teachers' expectations were high because there was ongoing progress monitoring, which included teacher–administration talks regarding data. Teachers were encouraged and empowered to set the bar at or above grade-level expectation but never below." High expectations were set during faculty meetings and by looking at the school's mission and vision as well. Students, however, did not recite affirmations schoolwide, although this was a practice in some teachers' classrooms.

When asked about the challenges she faced while trying to make AYP during those years, Austin said there were "limited time and resources (human and material) to meet the needs of the ESE population within the school day while complying with state mandates, such as mandatory PE [physical education]."

CHAPTER REFLECTION

1. How important is it for teachers to truly believe in their students and for students to believe in themselves? Explain your rationale. Support your answer with examples from the research.

2. Define *self-efficacy*. Summarize what the research says about the importance of self-efficacy. How can you apply this research practically to students in the classroom? Give specific examples.

3. Compare and contrast the strategies used by the two case study schools attempting to promote high expectations. Which strategies did the

principal at Pine Grove Elementary use that caused his school to be advanced (and make AYP)?

4. List the top five correlate strategies that you could implement to boost the presence of this correlate in your school district, school, or classroom. Why did you choose them? How would you implement them? How would you assess their effectiveness?

5. What teaching strategies could you use to ensure high expectations for all students? Give two or three scenarios explaining your application of these strategies.

6. Identify three or four strategies you could use to improve a student's self-efficacy. Explain how you would apply each of these to a specific situation.

7. The research shows the link between a teacher's self-efficacy and that of his or her students' self-efficacy. How would you rate your own self-efficacy on a scale of 1–10, with 1 being the lowest score and 10 the highest? What specific steps could you take to boost your personal self-efficacy?

Clear and Focused Mission Correlate

The mission serves as a polestar, or guiding principle, for a school. Just as a ship sails toward but never actually reaches its guiding star, we too strive toward but never actually fulfill our mission. Why? Because as long as the world continues to change and evolve, our students' needs will change, and we will need to develop new ways to respond.

—A.M. Blankstein (2004, p. 72)

Correlate Definition   In the effective school, there is a clearly articulated mission of the school through which the staff share an understanding of and a commitment to the school's goals, priorities, assessment procedures, and accountability. The staff in effective schools accept responsibility for the students' learning of the essential curricular goals. (Lezotte & McKee, 2002, p. 17)

The school library was tightly packed with teachers from every grade level at a local New York City middle school, Junior High School 194 William Carr. As a first year teacher, I [Melissa Harts] was one of the many crammed next to a bookshelf and a display case. From each corner of the room, teachers shifted and squirmed in the hardwood chairs as they huddled around the standard rectangular tables. As the noise level rose, it seemed to stifle some of the air in the poorly ventilated room, which seemed stuffier than usual. The principal entered with the two assistant principals in tow, and a silence fell over the room.

As expected (based on the memorandum placed in everyone's mailbox), the principal stated that today's objective was simply to create a mission statement from the embers of the one that was long forgotten and never used. It was the one that was in the front of the teacher handbook, given out at the beginning of the school year and usually hidden somewhere on the teacher's classroom shelf, in a bottom desk drawer, or in the teacher's personal closet in the back of the classroom. The administration made it clear that today's meeting was to discuss the direction of the school, especially with the influx of students from diverse cultural backgrounds, the addition of inexperienced teachers, and the latest district requirements to add to the federal and state mandates received the year before.

To their surprise, teachers were placed in grade-level groups for meaningful discussions on the school's mission. This new format was a change from the "sit next to your friend and follow the bulleted agenda" routine they had been accustomed to for years. The teachers took on the role of students and cooperatively discussed why the school's mission statement had lost its usefulness, why the school needed a new direction, and what they thought that direction should be. Meanwhile, the administrators walked around, assuming the role of classroom teachers, and peered over the teachers' shoulders to make sure all were on task. At no time was there an explanation of why the mission statement was a crucial component to having an effective school. At no time was there any mention of what mission statements should look like. And at no time was there a discussion about how to write a mission statement. As the administrators framed it, the goal was only to write one, given that the old one no longer applied.

THE IMPORTANCE OF A CLEAR AND FOCUSED MISSION

The scenario at that middle school is routinely repeated at other schools when educators are asked to revise or revisit their mission statements. The task, although an important one, is sometimes not explained clearly, and the school community—teachers, support staff, administrators, and parent representatives—does not work together. The mission activity becomes just another thing to do that is not deeply connected to the foundation of the school district's purpose of providing equal education for all students. On the other hand, sometimes mission statements are revised to fit a change in the school's culture. On these occasions, there is a need to fine-tune the mission so that it meets the school's expectations. There are also those times when the mission statement is tweaked to keep the school moving in a forward direction; sometimes mission statements are completely revamped because there is a new principal who wants to see the school take a different course. Whatever the reason, there comes a time in every school's history when the mission statement is either written because it is a new school, rewritten because the school has undergone a change, or revisited because the state accreditation team is coming for an evaluation. The question then becomes whether the school community uses it and puts its tenets into practice to guide decisions that affect student achievement.

Frontline Perspective

The vision and mission do impact achievement.

—Elementary school teacher

Lezotte (1991, 1997, 2002) reminds us that proficient schools have clearly articulated and focused visions and missions shared by staff. Staff accept the responsibility for teaching all students the essential core curriculum. However, in advanced schools, staff members also embrace the responsibility for students' learning regardless of the students' background or skills. Having a clearly focused school vision and mission is paramount if staff are to hit the target of enabling all students to make adequate learning gains.

STRATEGIES FOR DEVELOPING AND FOLLOWING A CLEAR AND FOCUSED MISSION

Everyone has a part to play in the mission statement's success: school board members must keep the organization in alignment with the mission, the superintendent must dictate the initiatives needed to accomplish the mission, the district leaders must implement these mission-led initiatives at the school level, the principals must provide leadership to direct the school community on how to make the mission possible, the teachers must communicate and demonstrate for students how they can be empowered by the mission, the students must keep the mission in mind as they work on skills to accomplish it, and parents must support the mission in their homes by modeling, staying involved, and supporting the school's efforts. The following strategies highlight how these themes of enforcement, review, information delivery, leadership, broadcasting, and initiative are involved at all levels.

What Highly Effective Superintendents and District Administrators Do

For high-level administrators, one of the primary strategies to ensure that a clear and focused mission is followed in schools is through *enforcement*. It is necessary to take these steps:

- Ensure that the district's mission is in alignment with the NCLB federal mandate.
- Hold district and school-level administration accountable for the data and require strategies for increasing student improvement.
- Enforce yearly reflective team analysis from all stakeholders to make sure that initiatives are reflective of the district's mission.

Similarly, superintendents and other high-level administrators *review* on an ongoing basis.

- Purposefully review and revise the district's strategic plan in accordance with the district's mission.

- Support a detailed review process of the school improvement plan and ensure its alignment with the school vision.
- Include as a part of the principal's performance review an evaluation of the visibility of the school's mission.
- Make sure the district's mission is visible on the district's web site, in the front office, and on district publications.
- Insist on district-level data review teams to monitor data and to ascertain whether they are consistent with the district's mission.

Finally, it is up to these administrators to ensure that they and the schools they support are *informed*. Strategies to make sure this is the case include the following:

- Request a copy of the requirements for the Clear and Focused Mission from the state's accreditation team. Make sure all components are incorporated in the district's mission review process.
- Provide feedback and a statistical look (i.e., data) at the effectiveness of the school district (particularly as it relates to the operationalization of the high-yield AYP predictor correlates).

What Highly Effective
Principals and School Administrators Do

Principals and school administrators in highly effective schools establish *requirements* to ensure the organization is united around its mission and vision. Specific strategies to do this are as follows:

- Require the school's mission statement to be featured in school mailings (e.g., newsletters, report cards, progress reports) and on the school's web site.
- Revisit the school's mission and vision statements periodically, and align school policies, procedures, and resultant decisions.
- Hold instructional leaders accountable for including a reflection or discussion of how the mission is being accomplished at the end of team or grade-level meetings.

At a deeper level, these leaders must *ensure* that schools follow through:

- Develop and periodically revise a Correlate-Based Strategic Improvement Plan (CBSIP; see Appendix 6.1 for an example).
- Design ways students can model the mission statement.

Principals and school administrators support the success of a mission statement by using their leadership role to promote it. Specific strategies include the following:

- Create professional learning communities at every grade level that reflect and report on how well the school is accomplishing its mission.

Frontline Perspective

The school's mission statement appears in all our correspondence, report cards, progress reports, and PowerPoint presentations, and is displayed in our reception area.

—Middle school assistant principal

- Broadcast and make visible the school's mission at every opportunity, including parent association meetings, staff meetings, school assemblies, and morning announcements and through available media such as the web site, school letterhead, TV, and (electronic) school billboards.

What Highly Effective Teachers Do

Teachers have the most direct contact with students and parents, and they *broadcast* the mission to these stakeholders when they use these strategies:

- Include the school's mission on the class web site and all other classroom communications.
- Use parent orientations to communicate the vision and mission.
- Celebrate the school vision and mission (a school celebrates what it values).
- Post the school's mission (and reflective class mission) in the classroom.

Frontline Perspective

I strive to demonstrate [our mission] through my actions in the classroom.

—Elementary school teacher

Teachers can also *initiate* new ways to involve the mission in students' day-to-day lives, making it more relevant and meaningful. These teachers

- Create classroom projects that allow students to demonstrate their understanding of the school's mission statement
- Have students take ownership of the mission statement by asking them to create personal learning goals for the school year

Frontline Perspective

Students can experience some success at the higher levels of education if they believe in the school's mission and vision statements.

—High school teacher

- Conduct individual student meetings quarterly to ensure that students are on track with their personal learning goals, which should be in alignment with the school's overall mission

Finally, teachers *inspect* student knowledge of the mission and their own use of it when they

- Require students to learn the mission statement
- Make sure that lesson plans include learning objectives that are reflective of the school's mission

Supportive Research

Despite the correlate definition for Clear and Focused Mission, the question still remains as to *what is the mission*. In the opening example of the New York City middle school, the teachers did not get a clear explanation of what a mission statement is, why is it a crucial component to having an effective school, and how to write an effective mission statement. This is an important starting point to understanding the relationship between the mission statement, school learning, and a school achieving AYP.

What Is a Clear and Focused Mission? Mission statements are abundant and can be researched on the Internet, located in business plans, or found in school improvement plans (SIPs). A comparison of several mission statements will show that they come in a variety of forms: some are a series of words that form an easy-to-remember acronym, some are in bulleted list form, others are two or more sentences in length. The word *mission* also has myriad definitions in both the public and private sectors. Covey (1989) says the mission sets the pace of the organization or the individual, adding, "It takes deep introspection, careful analysis, thoughtful expression, and often many rewrites to produce it in final form" (p. 129). The mission is also comparable to a goal or the sole purpose for the organization. Bennis and Goldsmith (2003) say that "it has to have meaning and resonance. It has to belong to everyone in the organization" (p. xv). Robbins and Alvy (2004) add that the mission statement serves as a "galvanizing force for staff, students, and community" (p. 9). Jones (1996) says there are three elements to a good mission statement: 1) it should be a single sentence long, 2) it should be easily understood by a 12-year-old, and 3) it should be able to be cited from memory at gunpoint. To support her simple and somewhat comical points, Jones offers this example:

> At a recent leadership seminar, I asked the 120 managers in attendance who could recite the mission statement of their company by memory. The company spent a small fortune in developing its mission statement, as evidenced by the elaborate, four-color, twelve page brochure, which I had received in advance of the seminar. Of the 120 leaders

there, only one could recite the mission statement. It was not the CEO. (p. 5)

For the purpose of this book, the mission statement should be considered a living document that gives the school organization a collective sense of purpose. It should be looked upon as a work in process that can be changed as the needs of the district or school community change. That is not to say that the mission statement should be taken lightly and tossed aside daily like a change of clothes. But it *is* to say that the mission statement should be the lens through which educators view their school, and a lens adjustment should be allowed if a strong need arises.

Experiences with mission statements range from seeing meaningless words posted on the walls at area schools to hearing students mumble convoluted paragraphs during a school presentation. However, in an effective school, says Blankstein (2004), the mission statement is the "vital lifeblood of the school's daily activities and policies" (p. 72.) An effective mission statement expresses the school's purpose—its essential reason for educating in the first place. It expresses why a school exists (Blankstein, 2004). Eaker, DuFour, and DuFour (2002) say the mission statement should address three critical questions: 1) If we expect all students to learn, what is it we expect them to learn? 2) How will we know if they are learning it? and 3) What will we do when they don't? Blankstein (2004) adds a fourth: How will we engage students in their own learning? This fourth question also ties into the correlate Climate of High Expectations, because the school would then emphasize the importance of student engagement in the learning process.

It is important to understand that an effective mission statement sets the framework of what is happening daily at the school. Each word should be carefully chosen with the understanding that the school community must all move in the same direction to increase student achievement. This direction must include certain stops along the way: 1) differentiating the curriculum to meet the learners' needs; 2) monitoring the data to ascertain where students are at a snapshot in time; 3) focusing on assessments and other evaluations; 4) reassessing, regrouping, and reteaching academic skills as needed; 5) offering remediation and other extended learning opportunities to close the learning gaps; and 6) using research-based and practical strategies to engage every level of learner.

The mission statement, then, should be simple, yet specific enough to address the learner, the instruction, and the commitment to learning for all. Then, daily goals and activities must be implemented that reinforce the mission, which moves the school forward. Simply stated, the mission is a roadmap for the school. If the school is compared to a car, then the mission is the map that leads the car to its destination. If for some reason, there is a missing sign or difficulty with the weather that causes a change in the route, the mission map still leads the way. It may have to be tweaked given the circumstances in order to get to the destination, but the map remains a viable component to getting the car where it needs to go.

What Is the Difference Between Vision and Mission Statements?

Before delving into why mission statements are so important in effective schools, it is important to clarify the difference between a vision statement and a mission statement. Hirsh (1996) clearly makes a distinction between the vision and the mission: the mission statement is a succinct, powerful statement on how the school will achieve its vision. Robbins and Alvy (2004) explain that at the vision is a core value or belief, "a descriptive statement of what the school will be like at a specified time in the future" (Hirsh, in Robbins & Alvy, p. 8). Therefore, the vision looks at what the district or school will be in the future, and the mission looks at what it has to do to get there today; the vision includes what all parties hope to do or become as a district or school community, and the mission tells them the steps they must take to make that hope a reality. In other words, the vision is the *what*, the mission is the *how*; the vision is the cake, the mission is the recipe. Most districts have both vision and mission statements that set the tone and the direction for the schools. Lashway (1997) holds that a vision (and mission) have several positive effects on a school: they attract commitment and energize people, create meaning in workers' lives, establish a standard of excellence, and bridge the present and the future.

The examples that follow were randomly chosen to show the distinction between vision and mission statements. They are not listed in a preferential order or as references for comparisons. These examples are from district and school web sites.

Lake Washington School District: Peter Kirk Elementary (2010)

> Vision Statement: Every Student Future Ready
> Mission Statement: Peter Kirk is a creative learning environment where children feel they are valued and safe. Staff and community collaborate to provide the highest quality education to prepare students to be lifelong learners.

Missouri Public Schools (Missouri Department of Elementary and Secondary Education, 2010)

> Vision Statement: Missouri Public Schools: the best choice . . . the best results!
> Mission Statement: The mission of the Missouri Department of Elementary and Secondary Education is to guarantee the superior preparation and performance of every child in school and in life.

So, as depicted in the examples, the vision and the mission statements have two distinct functions, but both are needed. Therefore, they work in tandem and keep the district and the school moving in a forward direction toward continuous improvement and student academic achievement (see Appendix 6.1).

Why Is the Mission Statement Important? The mission explains the way in which the school will get to the destination of learning for all. There may be stops along the way and changes in the route, but the mission provides the direction to show learning gains and improve overall student achievement. The mission statement is directly connected to the district's strategic plan or the school's SIP and permeates throughout every district or school initiative. It is important because it dictates the course of action that the school community will take in order to strengthen instructional strategies and learning experiences that directly affect student achievement.

Frontline Perspective

Student achievement is linked to the vision and mission of each school.

—District math coach

However, in and of itself, the mission statement is just a collection of words unless it is truly implemented in the fabric of the district or school community. There must be a collective belief in the fundamental points that drives instruction, supports progress monitoring, connects teacher professional development, and seeps into conversations with parents about their child's academic goals and overall improvement. The mission statement has to live in the hearts of all educators, students, and parents as they walk into the building. It must stay in their minds even after they leave.

Unfortunately, such is not the case in many public schools. The mission statement becomes a project that was completed years ago and is never made reference to after that. If someone bothers to take the time to look for it, it might be found posted somewhere in the front office or the cafeteria. Sometimes it is on the first or second page of teacher handbooks that are cracked open only if needed. It may be in bold font and fancy letters scrolled across web pages, but if you randomly ask a student, teacher, parent, or even district administrator to recite it, you may be quickly disappointed. In order for school districts and schools to be effective as they strive to improve student achievement, everyone must be in the same car, in alignment with the same mapped-out mission, and heading in the same direction. In addition, in order for the school community to remain focused on the importance of the mission, the mission statement has to be *visible* as well as *viable*. It must be readily accessible and posted everywhere as a reminder to all stakeholders.

If the vision and mission statements can be looked at as integral parts of the school community, then conversations can begin about how to re-design district-led initiatives to make them more effective, how to re-create lessons to increase student knowledge and skills, how to use assessments as an effective learning tool rather than a punitive measurement, and how to create a climate where learning is at the forefront of everyone's mind, from the school board member to the school bus driver. That's when the vision and mission statements become important—when there is a shared culture that respects and acknowledges its vital purpose.

A Culture of Shared Vision and Mission   Creating this culture of a shared vision and mission takes time and commitment. As Barth (1990) says, it is a formidable job to encourage teachers and principals to work together to consider, reflect on, and articulate their visions about what their schools might become. But it is the heart of school improvement. A culture where all stakeholders are moving fluidly with the mission creates an environment where learning for all is not just an expectation; it is a constant reality. The culture takes its shape in the teacher lounge discussions, during faculty meetings, at school board workshops, in district-level planning sessions, and in students' homes. However, creating and establishing a culture of shared vision and mission is not as easy as it may seem. When the vision and mission are not shared by the school community, there is a lack of focus, and the organization becomes unaligned and can be chaotic. There is no sense of purpose and priorities do not make sense.

For effective schools, there is a culture of shared vision and mission that sets them apart from ineffective schools. In effective schools, the staff accept responsibility for the students' learning and they work as a team of educators to ensure the students' academic success. Lezotte (2009) said,

> When we first started doing research on effective schools, we took as a given that schools had a shared understanding of what their mission was and ought to be. The more I work with schools, the more I become convinced that the issue of mission is one that must receive substantial discussion. When you think about all the things that might be done in the name of good education and realize the limits of your time, people power, energy, it becomes clear that there has to be some focus to the overall effort. This idea of a shared sense of mission is one way to assure that we're all moving in the same direction. One way to ascertain whether your school has a clear focus is to ask each stakeholder "What does this school care most about?" Would you get the same answer from each individual asked, or many different answers? To the extent that there are many answers, the school would be said to lack a shared sense of mission. (p. 8)

How to Create a Shared Culture of Vision and Mission   Of course, before creating a culture of shared vision and mission, the district and/or school must first define what its vision and mission are. Zmuda, Kuklis, and Kline (2004) say the first step is identifying and clarifying the core beliefs, which requires sustained conversation among the representatives of all members of the school community. This may be in the form of a PTA meeting, a School Advisory Council presentation, a school board meeting or workshop, or a faculty and staff presentation to the community. No matter what the written vision and mission statements turn out to be, the purpose of every school and district should be to maximize student achievement and to increase learning opportunities for all students.

deFur and Korinek (2006) have a list of books on developing professional learning communities that drive school improvement. In these professional learning communities, teachers develop strategies on how to continue to move forward in creating enriching cooperative learning lesson plans, developing valid assessments, and communicating the school vision and mission in every aspect of their instruction. When administrators create the environment for discussion about the vision and mission, encourage teachers to meet in professional learning communities, and provide support for schoolwide improvement in instruction and parental communication, then a culture of shared vision and mission can be established that becomes a part of every aspect of the school. An example of a principal's welcome back letter influenced by a school's shared vision and mission is included in Appendix 6.2.

Frontline Perspective

Use daily announcements, bulletin boards, and other sources to keep stakeholders informed of the vision and mission.

—Middle school principal

Once the culture for a shared mission and vision are established, then it must be cultivated and maintained. Administrators have to groom instructional leaders who model the vision and mission and continuously remind all stakeholders of its importance. Once this is happening in a school, then the school community will have a clear and focused mission, with every teacher, parent, volunteer, and support staff member aboard, following the map and heading in the same direction toward student growth and achievement.

SUMMARY

The mission statement is the key to setting the direction for educating students throughout the district and ultimately in every school. This mission statement, though, must come alive in the hearts and minds of those working daily to teach students, push them to higher levels of achievement, and give them a sense of a higher purpose for their lives. It must pulsate in the classrooms so that it keeps students, teachers, principals, and support staff all marching to the same beat, moving toward making learning gains in all academic areas. So many times, schools become bogged down in the day-to-day details, forgetting the mission that should drive instructional decisions and strategies. It is imperative that educators not forget the importance of the mission and learn how to cipher through the federal mandates, sift through the state and districtwide changes, and still remain focused on the goal to help their school make the grade.

As Blankstein (2004) states in the quote that begins this chapter, the mission is the polestar or guiding principle for a school. If educators do not concentrate on the guiding principle, ensuring that every child learns, then they might as well no longer be educators. It is the duty of educators to revisit their mission statements, reignite them, and move forward with the torch of purpose to help all students not only make learning gains and AYP (and help schools make the grade) but also to point the way for them to become empowered lifelong learners who will make a notable difference in society for years to come.

CASE STUDY
SCHOOL 1

At Pine Grove Elementary, the school community revisited its mission statement when a new principal took over the leadership. Although Principal Dave Dannemiller admired his predecessor, he had his own ideas about the new direction he wanted the school to take. Dannemiller recalled how his predecessor had opened the school and then moved on to open another school, taking half of the teachers with him. When Dannemiller became principal, he was left with the remaining half and he had to hire new teachers. His challenge was great in unifying the school and redefining its mission under his new leadership. He said that although redefining the school's mission was challenging because he had to create buy-in, the process was pivotal to laying the foundation for the school to improve student achievement and make AYP.

According to the 2008–2009 SIP for Pine Grove, the school's mission statement is as follows:

> To be our BEST! We strive to:
> B ecome an
> E mpowered and
> S elf-motivated community for
> T oday and tomorrow.

Reflecting on the beginning of his principalship, Dannemiller said, "That early part was a struggle and that was the time that we revisited the mission statement, why are we here, what's this all about, why do we come to work. That's when we started having common goals and moving forward." He added that he continuously had to remind the teachers, students, and staff that the mission had to be implemented daily. There were prominently placed signs announcing the mission statement posted around the campus. As mentioned earlier, the students said affirmations following the morning announcements to reemphasize the importance of the school's mission. There were conversations between teachers and administrators about data and how the mission related to making instructional strategies more effective to improve student achievement scores. These conversations trickled into teacher and parent discussions about student improvement.

Dannemiller added that after the school made AYP for the 2006–2007 school year, adhering to the mission became even more challenging because there was a perception that improvement was not needed. Recalling conversations with some of his teachers, Dannemiller said, "They would say, 'We're doing well now.' I'd say, 'There's always room for improvement. Let's look at this, let's look at that.' We had to keep things fresh and keep new ideas. We also had to keep the things that we were doing that worked. Everything we did centered around our mission and empowering our students to learn." Dannemiller said the mission drove the school community and helped everyone to stay focused. He suggested that the mission statement should be incorporated in every component of an effective school.

CASE STUDY
SCHOOL 2

Marcia Austin, former principal of John D. Floyd K-8 Environmental Science School, agrees with Dannemiller. The school's mission statement was revisited when it added a new environmental science middle school program. Although the mission statement was not changed, the focus of the environmental science program influenced the school's direction, because environmental science now had to be integrated throughout the curriculum. According to the 2008-2009 SIP for John D. Floyd K-8 School of Environmental Science, the mission statement is as follows:

> To promote a partnership with students, parents, and the community by providing a supportive educational environment enhanced by technology that encourages problem solving and responsible choices, thus preparing all to meet tomorrow's challenges.

Beginning in kindergarten, students at John D. Floyd are exposed to environmental science concepts that are built upon at every grade level. Austin said that the mission set the tone for "what was best for students and the organization." She said the school followed a mission to ensure excellence in education that permeated into the classroom. She said, "The heart of education is about students and all of us working together to nurture positive relationships in a collegial environment where all students can learn. At John D. Floyd, we did all we could to create a culture and climate of equity and excellence where all shared in the responsibility of educating all students."

The difference between the advanced school and the proficient school is that the mission statement at Pine Grove, the advanced school, was constantly infused into everything stakeholders did. Students had to memorize the mission statement, which was simple and effective. Teachers were reminded of the mission statement in everything that involved student learning and instruction. The administration was committed to ensuring that the mission statement was at the foundation of the school's drive toward excellence. At the proficient school, John D. Floyd, the mission statement was not a living part of the school environment, even though its premise was practiced.

CHAPTER REFLECTION

1. Discuss your response to the chapter prompt: "The mission serves as a polestar, or guiding principle, for a school" (Blankstein, 2004, p. 72). How can the mission guide the direction and activities of a school district, school, and classroom? Give specific examples.
2. Which strategies do you find to be most effective in creating a school culture of a shared mission and vision? Explain. Give two or three examples.
3. Jones (1996) says there are three elements to a good mission statement: 1) it should be a single sentence long, 2) it should be easily understood by a 12-year-old, and 3) it should be able to be cited from memory at gunpoint. Analyze your school vision and mission statement(s) in light of what Jones says. How does your school measure up? Rewrite your school mission based on the above criteria and other guidelines gleaned from this chapter.
4. What is the difference between a vision and mission statement? How could or should the school's vision and mission drive its strategic plan? Give examples. (Appendix 6.1 is a sample that will help with this response.)
5. How can the vision and mission become a daily guide for all activities? Give two or three examples. What key strategies could you implement to enable this outcome in your school district, school, or classroom?
6. Summarize what the chapter says about the importance of a Clear and Focused Mission. How does the presence of this correlate in a school

influence student academic achievement and help the school to make AYP? Give examples.

7. Review the Frontline Perspectives and the chapter strategies. List the top five strategies that you could implement to boost the presence of this correlate in your school district, school, or classroom. Why did you choose them? How would you implement them? How would you assess their effectiveness?

Appendix 6.1

Correlate-Based Strategic Improvement Plan (CBSIP) Worksheet

Creating a culture of a shared vision and mission takes time and commitment and should involve all key constituents. The following five questions are key conversation starters for schools interested in improving student achievement and can serve as prelude for the Correlate-Based Strategic Improvement Plan (CBSIP).

1. What is the one thing that this school should be remembered for?

2. What is the one thing that this school is not doing fully, that it should do to help **all** children further their education?

3. How do you think this one thing should be implemented?

4. What problems will need to be confronted to implement it?

5. Other Comments:

A CBSIP begins with the school's vision, mission, and core values and assesses each correlate based on a SWOT (Strengths, Weaknesses, Opportunities, and Threats) analysis. Goals, objectives, and action plans result. All of this is driven by a clear and focused school vision and mission. The SWOT analysis is a tool used to assist in strategic decision making and is generally attributed to Albert S. Humphrey (MarketingTeacher.com, n.d.).

VISION—A vision statement is future oriented. Write a comprehensive, future-oriented statement that shows what the school is aiming to do, educationally speaking.

_____

_____

_____

MISSION—A mission statement is now oriented. Write one statement that describes what the school is doing now in order to realize the vision or make it a reality now.

_____

_____

_____

COFFEE CUP VERSION (Keenan, n.d.)—This is a short three- to five-word phrase or sentence that captures the essence of your vision and mission statements. Review the vision and mission statements and write down your coffee-cup version.

_____

CORE VALUES—Pillars of belief that will not change regardless of time or circumstances. (The top Fortune 500 companies have solid core values that are unchanging over time.) Write down several. They should emanate from and resonate with your vision and mission statements (and vice versa).

1._____

2._____

3._____

4._____

5._____

SWOT ANALYSIS—This is an honest and open look at your school's strengths, weaknesses, opportunities, and threats at the current time through the correlate lens. Write down key SWOT items for each correlate listed in the table that follows and then prioritize them. (This plan could be adapted for a school, class, teacher, or student.)

S—Strengths: Write down the perceived positives of the correlates. Give examples of the evidence of each. Prioritize them.

_____

_____

_____

_____

W—Weaknesses: Write down the perceived negatives of the correlates. Give examples of the evidence of each. Prioritize them.

_____

_____

_____

_____

O—Opportunities: What are the potential opportunities for the improvement of each correlate? Think out of the box. Brainstorm opportunities for the improvement of each correlate. Give examples of each. Prioritize them.

_____

_____

_____

_____

T—Threats: What are the current perceived threats to the correlates? Give examples. Prioritize them.

_____

_____

_____

GOALS—Write down several broad goals based on your careful reflection of the SWOT analysis. A goal could be to improve a strength area, develop a weakness into a strength, realize an opportunity, or eliminate a threat. Prioritize your goals.

_____

_____

_____

_____

OBJECTIVES—Break down each goal into several manageable objectives or projects. Objective statements are one-line "to-do" statements that begin with the word *To*. Prioritize your objectives.

_____

_____

_____

_____

ACTION PLAN—The action plan precisely details your steps of action for each objective and includes a timeline and budget.

_____

_____

_____

_____

The CBSIP is an adaptation of the SWOT analysis approach to each correlate. By identifying each correlate's strengths, weaknesses, opportunities, and threats, educators can devise a strategic plan to help cultivate (or strengthen) the presence of each correlate. A strong presence of the correlates is associated with high academic achievement. (*Note:* Xs in the chart that follows indicate that a response is not necessary. For example, the *X* where Vision and Positive Home–School Relations intersect means it is not necessary to write a separate vision for this correlate—or the other correlates. It is sufficient to write a vision for the school as a whole.)

REVIEW—Periodically review and update your CBSIP.

BROADCAST—Keep the CBSIP visible before you, especially the vision and mission.

Strategist W.J. Cook, Jr., claimed, "Nothing creative happens until energy is forced into a discipline" (2000, p. 155).

Correlate-Based Strategic Improvement Plan (CBSIP) Worksheet

Strategic Plan	Correlates	Positive Home–School Relations	Opportunity to Learn and Student Time on Task	Climate of High Expectations	Clear and Focused Mission	Frequent Monitoring of Student Progress	Instructional Leadership	Safe and Orderly Environment
School Vision	Future	X	X	X	X	X	X	X
School Mission	Now	X	X	X	X	X	X	X
School Coffee-Cup Version of Vision and Mission Statements	3–7 word phrase	X	X	X	X	X	X	X
School Core Values	Pillars of belief that will not change	X	X	X	X	X	X	X
Correlate Strengths	X	1. 2. 3.	1. 2. 3.	1. 2. 3.	1. 2. 3.	1. 2. 3.	1. 2. 3.	1. 2. 3.
Correlate Weaknesses	X	1. 2. 3.	1. 2. 3.	1. 2. 3.	1. 2. 3.	1. 2. 3.	1. 2. 3.	1. 2. 3.
Correlate Opportunities	X	1. 2. 3.	1. 2. 3.	1. 2. 3.	1. 2. 3.	1. 2. 3.	1. 2. 3.	1. 2. 3.

Correlate Threats	X	1. 2. 3.	1. 2. 3.	1. 2. 3.	1. 2. 3.	1. 2. 3.	1. 2. 3.	1. 2. 3.
Correlate-Based School Goals	X	1. 2. 3.	1. 2. 3.	1. 2. 3.	1. 2. 3.	1. 2. 3.	1. 2. 3.	1. 2. 3.
Correlate-Based Objectives (for each goal)	X	1. 2. 3.	1. 2. 3.	1. 2. 3.	1. 2. 3.	1. 2. 3.	1. 2. 3.	1. 2. 3.
Correlate-Based Action Plan (for each objective)	X	1. 2. 3.	1. 2. 3.	1. 2. 3.	1. 2. 3.	1. 2. 3.	1. 2. 3.	1. 2. 3.

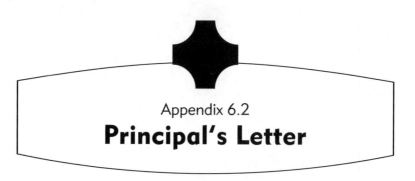

Appendix 6.2

Principal's Letter

The new principal of John D. Floyd K–8 Environmental Science School exemplified a shared culture of vision and mission in the welcome back letter he posted on his school's web page in August 2008. The letter shows that the culture has been nurtured to the point where all stakeholders are taking responsibility for accomplishing the mission. A copy appears here with permission.

Dear Parents,

A new school year is upon us; let me take this opportunity to welcome each student and parent to the 2008/2009 John D. Floyd K–8 School of Environmental Science community. As your new principal, I am honored to be able to serve the John D. Floyd family and feel as if I am returning home as I was here some twenty years ago as a guidance counselor. We have much to celebrate respective to our school grade "A". However, while we have accomplished much respective to State of Florida's grading system, we have failed to achieve AYP (Adequate Yearly Progress) as expected by the Federal Government's No Child Left Behind legislation.

Adequate Yearly Progress is a term designed to identify schools that have progressed to such a point that, according to the legislation, all students are proficient in all academic areas. John D. Floyd K–8 School of Environmental Science has not made Adequate Yearly Progress (AYP) despite making tremendous gains. Therefore, I will be initiating some new procedures to ensure that each student is given every opportunity to succeed.

One of the primary areas of concern toward making AYP is the area of reading. Every student will be expected to read four Accelerated Reader (AR)/Sunshine State books each nine weeks. Your continued support to promote recreational reading in your home would be greatly appreciated.

While we have demonstrated great growth in writing, much more progress needs to be realized. All students will be assessed monthly on their writing skills using the Florida Writes rubric. You can support our school community by having your child keep a journal on books they might read at home for pleasure. More information will be posted on our web site for clarification as to how to go about supporting a writing journal.

Another area of concern is for students who struggle academically with their core academic subjects. For the coming school year, any student who fails any core academic subject after the first nine weeks may be required to attend this after school tutorial assistance program until they secure a passing grade. Transportation will be available for students in need of such services. I recognize that this may be an imposition on some families; nevertheless, I need your support to ensure that every child succeeds.

Students' attendance and tardiness have been significant concerns to me throughout my professional career. Last school year I initiated a program for students who arrive late to class or for school. John D. Floyd's start time is 9:00 a.m.; I need you as parents to support the Floyd school community in expecting your child to be on time for school and on time to class. During this past school year, at least 50% of the students who were dropped off in the morning rode the bus home in the afternoon. I therefore encourage you to have your child ride the school bus to and from school in order to avoid tardiness.

John D. Floyd K-8 School of Environmental Science is committed to ensuring that every student is a success. Toward that end, we will be instituting a forty-five minute tutorial prior to any sports practice. Each sports coach will be assisting his/her team during a study hall which will be structured and supported by our school's Reading Leadership Team. This will provide students the opportunities for enrichment activities which will assist them on the FCAT. Any student athlete who has a failing grade after the first nine weeks will be expected to attend the after school tutorial program two days a week in lieu of attending the team practice until the next marking period.

Students who are struggling following the progress reports and nine week report card notification will be offered an opportunity to remain after school for additional tutorial assistance. More information will be posted on the school web page for clarification concerning this program.

The John D. Floyd school community has garnered a reputation as an outstanding educational facility. This reputation has come because of the high expectations our teachers and staff hold, as well as the high expectations you as parents have of our school faculty and staff. "Commitment to Excellence" is the cornerstone statement which the District uses to promote Hernando County Schools. Floyd's cornerstone statement will be "no excuses". We will offer you "no excuses" as to why we haven't done everything possible to assist every child, and we ask that you offer us "no excuses".

With Respect,

Joe Clifford
Principal

Frequent Monitoring of Student Progress Correlate

with Sonya Jackson

People do what you inspect, not what you expect.

—Lou Gerstner (2002, p. 231)

> **Correlate Definition**   In the Effective School, pupil progress over the essential objectives [is] measured frequently, monitored frequently, and the results of those assessments are used to improve the individual student behaviors and performances, as well as to improve the curriculum as a whole. (Lezotte & McKee, 2002, p. 18)

When I [Cheryl Edwards, an elementary teacher and adjunct education professor] started teaching, the pressure of improving the school grade and attaining AYP was tremendous. My teammates and I experienced first-hand the stress and worry that accompanies the glare of unwanted attention, followed by high-stakes testing. District-level administrators made daily visits to our campus, challenging the faculty with new and mandatory training. From the very beginning of the school year, our team met monthly to discuss student data from one subject and monitor student progress. This time together provided great communication between teammates and helped steer us into a common direction in order to meet the academic needs of our students.

From standardized tests from the fourth grade, our students clearly showed an overall weakness in mathematics. Therefore, we devised a plan during our meetings to assess our students with mathematical concepts and then to share their progress. Every month, we discussed our progress on the math scope and sequence calendar and what concepts seemed to be difficult to master. We gave sub-topic tests, along with topic tests throughout the first semester. Then, we gave a practice [cumulative] test which was instrumen-

tal in the creation of our differentiated instruction plan. We did an item-by-item analysis and figured out which problems were missed most often and correlated those problems to the actual strand. Through collaborating with each other, we decided to divide the children into small groups by ability. We created a common assessment of what was taught throughout the week. Each teacher was responsible for writing five test questions that resembled the ones on the standardized test. We combined the questions and gave the test in each base class. After grading the assessment, we then took a class average and posted this in the classroom.

We witnessed tremendous growth and the students began taking ownership of their scores. When the annual standardized test results were published, our fifth grade team sat back with amazement! It was wonderful! Our school not only earned a grade of an "A", but more importantly, we earned AYP for the very first time.

THE IMPORTANCE OF FREQUENTLY MONITORING STUDENT PROGRESS

Frequent monitoring of student progress is a technique that provides continuous feedback to teachers about the effectiveness of the instructional program and the students' achievement. Frequent monitoring helps teachers use students' performance data to frequently assess the effectiveness of their teaching and formulate more educated instructional decisions (Safer & Fleischman, 2005).

NCLB requires teachers to monitor the progress of students who fall below standards by providing benchmark assessments, comparing results, implementing instructional strategies to show learning gains, and applying response to intervention techniques such as effective instruction in general education, data-guided decisions, targeted intervention strategies for at-risk students, and integrated services for all students. In sync with Lezotte's (1997) report of progress monitoring in "first- and second-generation" schools, proficient schools frequently monitor all student learning

Frontline Perspective

I scrutinize student progress on a weekly basis. I review grade summaries and monitor individual gains/losses in all subject areas.

—Elementary school teacher

and make adjustments as needed, whereas advanced schools also use technology to enable teachers to monitor student progress and students to monitor their own progress.

STRATEGIES TO IMPROVE MONITORING OF STUDENT PROGRESS

Data on student progress is regularly reviewed at different levels of the school system, and thus each level has its role to play. The underlying themes of these strategies for frequent monitoring of student progress include authorization, analysis, development, leadership, disaggregation, communication, monitoring, implementation, and interaction.

What Highly Effective
Superintendents and District Administrators Do

The first strategy for upper-level administrators is to *authorize* use of personnel and systems that will support the ongoing progress monitoring effort. These administrators

- Allocate an assessment team that oversees district progress monitoring and results, and appoint an assessment liaison at each school who reports directly to the district assessment supervisor
- Require schools to submit progress monitoring results on students in the bottom quartile with strategies that are being implemented to increase student learning

   As overseers of large amounts of data, district leaders play a vital role in *analyzing* this data. Highly effective administrators

- Invest in technology assessment tools and personnel to quickly disaggregate the data
- Conduct quarterly data review meetings with school teams to track assessment results
- Implement district executive team meetings that foster reflective conversations with directors of special education, curriculum, assessment, and technology
- Inform all staff and the community of student performance
- Analyze districtwide and individual school scores along with staff, use the data to make inferences about program success, and target new areas for school improvement

   Leaders encourage districtwide progress monitoring by *developing* supports for the lower levels. They

- Ensure that the district and school leadership teams understand the importance of frequent monitoring and its impact on student achievement results
- Provide professional development opportunities in frequent monitoring strategies and techniques such as data disaggregation, aligning rubrics with assessment, and alternative assessment techniques

- Support guidance counselors in providing clear assessment procedures and protocols

Finally, these administrators provide oversight of progress monitoring efforts. District-level administrators should make frequent visits to struggling campuses and challenge the faculty to master proven effective strategies that enhance student learning.

What Highly Effective
Principals and School Administrators Do

In the position of spearheading all assessments and progress monitoring at a school, the primary role of these administrators is to provide *leadership*. These individuals should take these steps:

- Become assessment literate and thus able to transform their expectations into assessment exercise and scoring procedures that accurately reflect student achievement (School Improvement in Maryland, 2009). Becoming assessment literate means taking the time to understand the indicators from the data, comparing the indicators with previous student assessment data, developing research-based interventions that can be used to remediate the student on the learning deficit, and consulting with a data review team to discuss results and integrate the intervention strategies throughout the instruction to strengthen the student's skills.

> **Frontline Perspective**
>
> We have instructional team meetings and grade-level meetings where we provide teachers with access to benchmark test scores.
>
> —Middle school principal

- Make monitoring of student progress (including tracking of learning gains) a priority.
- Strive to be the instructional leader, and hold teachers accountable for their use of data to improve student achievement.
- Require assistant principals and team leaders to work with teachers to disaggregate data and provide instructional strategies to increase student performance.
- Hold data review team meetings quarterly with teachers and chart progress from one quarter to the next.

> **Frontline Perspective**
>
> Each nine weeks, . . . we analyze the data and pull out the lowest 25%, and each administrator works with them one on one.
>
> —Middle school assistant principal

- Require teachers to hold workshops for parents on progress monitoring assessments to facilitate understanding of frequent monitoring and how it affects student achievement.

Similar to how administrators in a district can provide supports for schools, school administrators should also *develop* these supports for their staff:

- Provide training on how to monitor student progress, especially in the core subject areas.
- Encourage teachers to use technology to get quick snapshots of student performance to help support learning gains.
- Provide remediation and creative schedules for students in need of additional instructional time based on progress monitoring results.
- Set the school's direction, develop people, and develop the school.
- Analyze test data, grade distribution, and enrollment patterns by race, gender, ethnicity, and socioeconomic status to detect any inequity and to ensure that all students are learning.

What Highly Effective Teachers Do

When teachers assess for learning, they use formal classroom assessment data and anecdotal student data to advance student learning. Working directly with students on the ground level, so to speak, teachers first must *disaggregate* the information collected through progress monitoring to be able to make use of the data. They do the following:

- Collect and disaggregate relevant data on a frequent basis.
- Analyze data using visual means to interpret student progress.
- Conduct an item analysis to assess problem areas (and strengths). According to the Office of Educational Assessment (n.d.), this process "examines student responses to individual test items (questions) in order to assess the quality of those items and of the test as a whole" and "is valuable for increasing instructors' skills in test construction, and identifying specific areas of course content which need greater emphasis or clarity" (para. 1).
- Identify goals directly aligned with curriculum or student needs.
- Understand and articulate in advance of teaching the achievement targets that their students are to hit.
- Make instructional decisions based on careful interpretation of the data.

Teachers also must *communicate* about progress monitoring to ensure that students are involved in the process and that the process is meaningful. Teachers should take these steps:

- Inform their students about learning goals, in terms that students understand, from the very beginning of the teaching and learning process.
- Have conferences with students and show them the data results so that they can set goals and chart their own progress.
- Show students how to study and provide test-taking strategies that they can use to be successful.
- Understand that constant and immediate feedback is needed for instruction to have a positive impact on students.

Although data are reviewed by people at all levels of the school system, teachers are the ones in a position to have it directly affect their day-to-day work of instructing students. Teachers who actively *monitor* student progress are able to teach responsively and proactively. These teachers use the following strategies:

- Make sure that rubrics and alternative assessments are directly linked to the curriculum.
- Perform frequent monitoring and reflection on students who are in the lowest quartile and students at risk of falling into the lowest quartile.
- Know on a day-to-day basis where their students are in relation to content standards.
- Continuously adjust instruction based on the results of classroom assessments.
- Stay attuned to students' self-confidence, especially in testing.
- Translate classroom assessment results into frequent descriptive feedback for students, providing them with specific insights on how to improve.
- Engage students in regular self-assessments, with standards held constant so that students can watch themselves grow over time and thus feel in charge of their own success.

By the same token, it is the work of teachers to *implement* progress monitoring efforts. Teachers who do this most effectively take these actions:

- Provide differentiated instruction in lessons and keep all learning styles in mind when teaching.
- Are creative with assessments so that they adhere to the material and the student's learning style.

Frontline Perspective

I daily check homework for reading assignments. I give reading check quizzes occasionally....I give major unit tests and final exams.

—High school teacher

- Align assessments with the curricular aim and then implement instructional strategies.

- Are proactive in making instructional decisions to improve student learning.

- Use classroom assessment to build students' confidence in themselves as learners and help them take responsibility for their own learning, so as to lay a foundation for lifelong learning.

Frontline Perspective

I use scientifically based monitoring programs three times a year to assess my students' academic performance and to evaluate the effectiveness of my instruction.

—High school reading teacher

Finally, although much of the work of monitoring student progress is a task for the teacher to individually implement with his or her students, the effort should inform and be supported by *interactions* with administrators and parents. Great teachers use these approaches:

- Ask for help in understanding test results and what one can do to foster student achievement.

- Speak to parents about the importance of the data, what they are doing in the classroom to increase learning gains, and how parents can support these efforts at home.

- Actively involve students in communicating with their teacher and their families about their achievement status and improvement.

- Consult with an administrator immediately about students who are not making progress as expected.

Supportive Research

Effective leaders in effective schools are characterized by requiring frequent assessments of student progress. A variety of assessment methods such as teacher-made tests, criterion-referenced tests, and norm-referenced tests are utilized. The results of these assessments are used to improve the programs and to alter teacher strategies when needed. In effective schools, there is congruence between the objectives of the school's curriculum, what teachers teach, and the tests that are used (Lezotte, 1991).

Beginning with the End in Mind Covey (1989) explains that highly effective people begin with the end in mind. Popham (2007) concurs, urging teachers to begin their specific classroom instruction with the curricular aim in mind—that is, a clear target of what one is trying to achieve. He strongly advocates that teachers develop the assessment tool that directly reflects the curricular aims. The final step is to implement effective instructional strategies to teach the curricular aim. Popham holds that when the curricular aims, assessments, and strategies are in alignment—in that order—

instruction will be focused on the target, with corresponding increases in student academic achievement. He is quick to point out that most teachers begin with the curricular aims but then focus on the instructional strategies instead of creating the assessment by which students will be evaluated. In this approach, the assessment may not align closely with the curricular aims, and students may fail to excel (Popham, 2007).

Frontline Perspective

I monitor my students over time. I am always checking their grades and testing them on material that we had in prior semesters.

—Middle school teacher

According to the California Center for Effective Schools (2009), there is a clearly articulated school mission through which the staff share an understanding of and commitment to the instructional goals, priorities, assessment procedures, and accountability. According to the California Center for Effective Schools (2009), an effective school should demonstrate the following criteria, especially in relation to frequent monitoring of student performance:

- Achievement data form the basis for updates in instruction and processes.
- "Test data, grade distribution and enrollment patterns are analyzed by race, gender, ethnicity and socio-economic status to detect any inequity and to ensure that all students are learning " (para. 19).
- Student performance summaries are communicated to staff and the community. All staff examine scores for both the entire district and each school to determine which areas are successful and which require improvement.
- Teachers design and/or implement norm-referenced and/or authentic assessment methods to determine mastery of grade or course goals.

The only way for teachers and schools to identify which students can demonstrate proficiency on state content standards is to continuously assess and monitor students as part of their classroom instruction. Teachers must know on a day-to-day basis where their students are in relation to the content standards. This way the teachers will have the necessary information to implement effective instructional practices. In addition, the data generated from classroom assessments are used as comparisons to the quarterly schoolwide assessments that effective schools use to make needed decisions about curriculum, assessment, and instructional strategies across the school.

In order to do this, schools must first identify the student achievement data they need to collect to determine if they are making progress toward the attainment of their priority goals. According to deFur and Korinek (2006), an effective school accomplishes progress monitoring using the following four essential steps:

- **"Step 1: Identify goals directly aligned with curriculum or students' needs" (para 4).** Align with state standards and/or IEP goals so that data collection assesses student performance in the general education curriculum. This purpose should be in view when progress monitoring starts.
- **"Step 2: Collect relevant data on a frequent basis" (para. 5).** Assessments need to yield data that are linked to teacher and student accountability. Collecting data on a daily and weekly basis helps educators spot issues and either provide remedial or more challenging instruction as applicable. Various types of informal assessment (e.g., observations, student work samples, rubrics) allow regular data collection and improve instruction efficiency.
- **"Step 3: Analyze data using visual means to interpret student progress" (para. 6).** Progress should be illustrated through visual methods (e.g., graphs, charts) that show how student performance relates to standards. It is important not to simply gather data, as data collection has no bearing on student progress.

> **Frontline Perspective**
>
> *I use several different types of informal and formal assessments daily and throughout the unit. My informal assessments include warm up, closure, focus on vocabulary, and daily puzzler questions that the students sometimes complete independently and sometimes complete in collaborative pairs.*
>
> *—High school math teacher*

- **"Step 4: Make instructional decisions based on careful interpretation of the data" (para. 8)** Such decision making involves determining whether instruction should remain unchanged or whether certain curricular and instructional elements (e.g., interventions, methods) need updating.

Fifth grade language arts standards focus on writing for a variety of purposes, gathering information, integrating technology, and organizing information. Additionally, producing documents demonstrating completeness and understanding of focus, organization, support, and conventions satisfies required standards. The data derived from these formative or summative assessments can indicate successful student understanding. By approaching writing through real world, project-based tasks, today's teacher can still teach the "nuts and bolts" of grammar and assess using standard measures along with alternative assessments suitable for authentic projects.

One authentic task used in my class, after assessing existing writing data along with current class needs, was a class book project. Students wrote, illustrated, and published a bilingual parallel text class book that was available for purchase by parents. Monitoring and assessing student performance on

this project began with a KWL chart [a graphic organizer with columns listing what a student knows, wants to learn, and—after reading the material—finally has learned] about book publishing, rubrics for the oral presentation, written journal activity, and student/peer editing. Additionally, students received a holistic rubric to score individual classmates on their oral presentation. There was no assessment used for the artwork other than student completion. Students completed the KWL chart when the books arrived from the publisher, and an "exit ticket" answered three questions about the project regarding likes, dislikes, and any remaining questions. Incorporating writing into a variety of projects, I've come to understand that the goal of today's teacher is to tie together benchmarks and assessments into meaningful tasks that cross subject areas, involve inquiry, technology, and provide a personalized learning experience.
—Teacher's perspective by Patricia Doyle (Teacher of the Year 2008–2009, Pine Grove Elementary)

Why Is Monitoring Necessary?   Progress monitoring promotes student achievement. If teachers and leaders are ever to know how students are performing, they will need to know what students are scoring on tests. Progress monitoring allows teachers and administrators to have data results that can be predictors of how students will perform on standardized tests. Thus, in today's accountability-driven education model, progress monitoring is a crucial, proactive component to finding learning gaps in student achievement, creating prescriptive and individualized student learning plans, and developing instructional strategies school- and district-wide to foster student learning gains. If educators consistently and effectively monitor progress, they should know exactly where students are performing in reading comprehension, math standards, and writing at any point throughout the school year. They should know which students are proficient and which are not. They should have evidence for the students who are proficient and evidence for the students who are not performing at successful levels. As educators, they should have data to identify who these students are, and if they do not know who these students are, then they need to find out by progress monitoring subgroups more frequently.

With the litany of progress monitoring tools available in each of the subject areas, there is no excuse not to frequently monitor students. Annual data from state assessments only give schools a glimpse of where students

Frontline Perspective

This year for reading alone, in addition to traditional tests, I've had students record their reading on tape recorders and iPods, read to "student experts," keep checklists and KWLs, and complete projects independently and cooperatively.

—Elementary school teacher

are at a single point in time. Daily instruction continues between the time the state tests are given and the time the results are returned to schools. The results are dated and provide only a snapshot of where students were when they took the test. Teachers must know on a day-to-day basis where their students are in relation to the content standards to have the necessary information to inform instruction.

What Are the Benefits of Progress Monitoring?   According to the National Center on Student Progress Monitoring (2009),

> When progress monitoring is implemented correctly, the benefits are great for everyone involved. Some benefits include accelerated learning, because students are receiving more appropriate instruction; more informed instructional decisions; documentation of progress for student accountability purposes; more efficient communication with families and other professionals about students' progress; higher expectations for students by teachers; and fewer Special Education referrals. Overall, the use of progress monitoring results in more efficient and appropriately targeted instructional techniques and goals. These goals and techniques together move all students to faster attainment of important state standards of achievement. (para. 4)

Leadership, Frequent Monitoring, and Student Achievement   According to Brewster and Railsback (2005), principals play a critical role in school improvement. In reviewing the literature, Leithwood and Riehl (2003) reveal several key findings that suggest successful leaders influence student achievement by a core set of practices: setting directions, developing people, and developing the organization. In setting directions, the principal must identify and articulate a vision, create shared meanings, create high performance expectations, foster the acceptance of group goals, monitor organizational performance, and communicate. In developing people, the principal must offer intellectual stimulation, provide individual support, and provide an appropriate model. As the principal is developing the organization he or she must strengthen the school culture, modify organizational structure, build collaborative processes, and manage the environment (Leithwood & Riehl, 2003).

Leadership is second only to classroom instruction among all school-related factors that contribute to what students learn at school. Teachers are the core ingredient needed to make a difference in the data, because they directly influence student achievement. They should differentiate their instruction, work with teams of educators and colleagues to come up with strategies to help students learn and make learning gains, and communicate with students and parents about their test results and what can be done at home to help support student achievement. They should provide timely and meaningful feedback to students. Parents should request to see progress monitoring results on their child, stay informed about testing and assessments done at the school, and provide support at home that encourages learning and academic achievement.

Finally, and most important, students need to set goals for themselves based on their assessments. They must *want* to do well and must do everything within their power to achieve that goal. This includes studying, paying attention in class, asking questions, doing homework and assignments, and above all else, never settling for anything less than their best. If everyone does his or her part in monitoring student progress, then students will be well on their way to making substantial learning gains that will lead to success, not only in school but thereafter as well. The operationalization of the Frequent Monitoring of Student Progress correlate will also be reflected in increased AYP scores—and that is what schools need and want.

SUMMARY

In this era of accountability, it is imperative that educators frequently monitor student progress and use the data to drive instruction. Although this may seem like a daunting process, it does not have to be if everyone is involved in collecting the data, analyzing it, and making sound decisions that will lead to student achievement. The district should set the tone by supporting assessment teams, providing resources and programs to help schools make needed decisions that can result in student academic growth, and helping disaggregate data expeditiously so that information can be disseminated to the schools.

Remember the chapter quote: "People do what you inspect, not what you expect" (Gerstner, 2002, p. 231). The principal must hold his or her assistant principals, team leaders, and teachers accountable for the data. He or she must make sure that teachers are frequently monitoring students and that all assessments are in alignment with the curriculum. Teachers must provide feedback to students, and parents should stay informed about testing and assessments and support their child's learning. Finally, students must set goals for themselves based on their assessments and closely monitor their own progress. Frequent monitoring helps schools make the grade.

CASE STUDY

SCHOOL 1

At Pine Grove Elementary, the teachers monitored data and explored ways to improve student test scores. Dave Dannemiller, the former principal, said that through progress monitoring he was able to produce reports that showed how each individual student was doing in core academic areas. "Using the Successmaker program [Pearson Education, 2009], in reading and math, we were running a 95%–98% correlation to the performance on that program, which is comparable to a level 3 or higher FCAT score," he said. "I would stress to these teachers, 'What better tool do you have than when you have a 98% confidence rate that if the student gets to this point he will have a level 3 or higher?' It also tracks if the kids are falling short of that mark." He said that he followed up on the data by bringing teachers into his office to discuss struggling students based on the data. "I would say, 'OK what are you doing to help the student to show learning gains? Here are some things that you can do. Why don't you show me this so that I can see how the student is progressing?' I was very fortunate that the last couple of years of making AYP, I saw a shift where that discussion didn't have to take place and teachers were coming to me, telling me what they were doing and asking me for suggestions."

Dannemiller said that when he saw the shift in teachers being proactive in making instructional decisions to improve student learning, he knew that he had built a culture where frequent monitoring was a key ingredient used to improve student scores. "That was magical," he said. "I felt that I had reached an objective. Teachers became self-motivated and took responsibility for the data. They began to see it for themselves, and they knew that I knew, so it wasn't like they were throwing themselves under the bus. They would say, 'I know you saw this. What can I do?'"

CASE STUDY
SCHOOL 2

Similar discussions were heard in the classrooms, administrative offices, and teacher lounges at John D. Floyd K-8 Environmental Science School. Teachers also monitored progress using assessment software and online applications such as the Dynamic Indicators of Basic Early Literacy Skills (DIBELS; University of Oregon, Center on Teaching and Learning, n.d.) and developing ThinkLink (Discovery Education, 2007) probes in math and reading. Across each grade level, there were required data review meetings for teachers to discuss student progress, instructional strategies, and recommendations for continued improvement. Teachers had a flow chart and checklist that included parent contact, feedback from guidance counselors, data review with the school assessment team, data review with the grade-level math or reading coach, and required quarterly review meetings with administration on individual students, especially those in the bottom quartile at the school.

The former principal, Marcia Austin, said frequent monitoring was an expected routine at the school. She said, "There were two layers of frequent monitoring. In the classroom, the teachers were expected to analyze test results and take appropriate action. In the assessment/administration office, grade distribution reports and benchmark assessment were analyzed." She said that frequent monitoring was everyone's responsibility at the school, and administrators built a culture where teachers took ownership for their own student data. "There were multiple monitoring practices in place: 1) weekly monitoring of the high-risk population in the primary grades; 2) frequent and common classroom assessments; 3) benchmark assessments; and 4) analysis and reflection of the results," she said, adding that data reflection is a key component to frequent monitoring because it forces the teacher to ask questions about what is working and what is not.

For the Frequent Monitoring of Student Progress correlate, both schools were effective advanced schools (Lezotte, 1997), because the teachers used technology to monitor students' progress. Students could track their own progress and keep student improvement portfolios. Also encouraged at both schools were data walls where teachers displayed overall student growth and gains without identifying student names. These progress monitoring practices created a culture at both schools where data were an integral part of demonstrating proven results of student learning. Finally, the principals at both schools created a culture where progress monitoring was routine and an expected component of the students' learning plan.

CHAPTER REFLECTION

1. Discuss your response to the chapter prompt: "People do what you inspect, not what you expect" (Gerstner, 2002, p. 231). Are there pros and cons to progress monitoring? Give specific examples.

2. Proficient schools frequently monitor student learning and make adjustments as needed, whereas advanced schools also use technology to monitor student progress. Give two or three examples of how teachers and students in advanced schools might use technology to monitor learning. Are there any limitations in the use of technology? Explain.

3. How could you build a school culture that promotes the Frequent Monitoring of Student Progress correlate? Give two or three specific examples from the chapter.

4. Comment on the following statement: "In effective schools, there is congruence between the objectives of the school's curriculum, what teachers teach, and the tests that are used" (Lezotte, 1991) in light of Popham's (2007) assertion that effective teachers should teach to the curricular aims after formulating assessments based on those aims. Is alignment (or congruence) of these three elements really that important in boosting student learning as measured by state standardized test scores? Explain, giving two or three examples.

5. Identify the steps you would take as a district-level administrator, school principal, or teacher to use data to improve instruction and therefore student achievement. Give a brief scenario of how these steps could be implemented.

6. List several key strategies mentioned in the chapter that you could use to boost the presence of the Frequent Monitoring of Student Progress correlate in your school district, school, or classroom. Why did you choose them? How would you implement them? How would you assess their effectiveness?

7. What is your favorite Frequent Monitoring of Student Progress strategy? Why?

Instructional Leadership Correlate

with Scott Bryan

Involvement in Curriculum, Instruction, and Assessment is considered critical to the concept of instructional leadership

—R.J. Marzano, T. Waters, and B.A. McNulty (2005, p. 53)

Correlate Definition   In the effective school, the principal acts as an instructional leader and effectively and persistently communicates the mission of the school to staff, parents, and students. In addition, the principal understands and applies the characteristics of instructional effectiveness in the management of the instructional program. (Lezotte & McKee, 2002, p. 16)

I [Scott Bryan, former Superintendent of Schools, Indiana, and current Associate Professor of Education, Southeastern University, Florida] served in Indiana's schools for nearly 3 decades, the last 9 years as superintendent. Prior to that, I served in the capacity of Assistant Superintendent for 7 years in charge of Curriculum, Assessment, and Instruction. I managed and developed the curriculum for all the K–12 subject areas and mapped the expectations for each grade level/subject area, identified resources needed, and targeted effective instructional strategies. Curriculum, instruction, and assessment have remained areas of particular focus for research and development.

I believe that people think you value where they see you spend your time. Therefore, I established three major goal areas as superintendent. They included coordinating curriculum development/instruction/student achievement, developing and maintaining excellent facilities, and maintaining sound fiscal management. Instructional leadership was my number one priority, as evidenced by the amount of time I spent focusing on student performance data. It also became the district's priority goal. I find support for this priority in research conducted by Marzano (2003). He states that the number one factor influencing student academic achievement is the school's focus on curriculum. The number one factor that teachers should focus on to improve student achievement is developing their instructional strategies.

125

I championed the cause of curriculum and instructional leadership in my district through various means. For example, I included an agenda item related to curriculum on each monthly school board meeting agenda. During the winter months we conducted our school board meetings (on a rotational basis) at the various school buildings during the school day. Teachers and students made presentations during the school board meetings to highlight special programs and areas of interest. Additionally, it helped create teacher and staff buy-in to the importance of instructional leadership.

I held meetings with principals on a monthly basis. Training sessions on data disaggregation and using data to drive instruction across the curriculum were presented throughout the year. These proved to be invaluable sessions since principals had generally been trained to use Excel in school management but had not been equipped in the science of data-driven instruction. I felt it was important for principals to take the lead in this area and set the tone for their schools. During our principal meetings we analyzed data from every grade level and subject area. We were constantly looking at the data, looking for what was working, and identifying what needed to improve. Principals were held accountable for student learning gains, and one component of their annual performance review was tied to the student performance.

Principals would, in turn, coach teachers in the finer aspects of data-driven decision-making. They would hold their teachers accountable for student learning. Each school in the district analyzed data from a number of sources. These included a baseline test (Northwest Testing) which targeted skills in Reading, Math, and Language Arts, the ISTEP state comprehensive test, and locally developed tests. The Northwest baseline test was given at the beginning of the year to assess students' academic levels and diagnose weaknesses, and again at the end of the year to track learning gains. The state comprehensive test (ISTEP) was given in the fall in order to allow teachers sufficient time to use the results for instructional purposes. Local testing was done throughout the year to supplement the other two tests and to drill down further once an area of weakness had been highlighted by them. The results of this triangulation approach to testing were carefully monitored and tracked using Excel spreadsheets. Teachers would meet and discuss the results and use the data to drive their classroom instruction.

In this era of NCLB accountability, it is important that educators align the curriculum with state standards and, in turn, instructional approaches with the curriculum. Assessments should be tied directly to curriculum and instruction. Assessment should be developed to answer the question, "What would I accept as evidence that the students understand?"

THE IMPORTANCE OF INSTRUCTIONAL LEADERSHIP

In proficient schools, the principal effectively and persistently communicates the school mission to staff, parents, and students. The principal is also cognizant of characteristics of instructional effectiveness and applies them. In the advanced school, the instructional leadership concept is broadened and leadership is viewed as including all adults, especially teachers. This is in keeping with the teacher empowerment model that recognizes that complex organizations such as schools have *distributed leadership:* that is, the principal is not the only leader in the school. The leadership approach focuses on creating a community of shared values. The principal's essential role is as a leader of leaders, which requires the principal to develop his or her skills as coach, partner, and cheerleader (Lezotte, 1997; Lezotte & McKee, 2002).

STRATEGIES FOR IMPROVING INSTRUCTIONAL LEADERSHIP

Teachers, principals, administrators, and superintendents are all leaders. At these different levels, they each have a role to play in supporting student learning. Themes that underscore the following strategies include prioritizing, analyzing, equipping, learning, modeling, building, disaggregating, growing, and evaluating.

Frontline Perspective

You've got to give them something to look for, something to strive for. . . . Make things easy and available for teachers . . . so that everyone is on the same page.

—*Elementary school principal*

What Highly Effective
Superintendents and District Administrators Do

As leaders at the top level, superintendents and district administrators set *priorities* that affect every school in the system. They show their commitment to instructional leadership when they take these steps:

*   Hire highly effective leaders, because they know that good schools have strong instructional leaders.
*   Make instructional leadership their number one priority.
*   Make the curriculum the focal point of learning and ensure that everybody is on board.
*   Include an agenda item related to the curriculum in each monthly school board meeting.
*   Conduct school board meetings at the various school buildings during the school day (keeps school board members in touch with schools).
*   Hold regular (monthly) meetings with principals; have sessions that focus on the disaggregation of data and using data to drive instruction across the curriculum.

With access to great amounts of data, it is important that administrators *analyze* it to extract useful and practical information. Highly effective superintendents and district administrators do the following:

- Analyze data from every grade level and subject area—with principals always looking for what is working and what needs to improve.
- Analyze data from a number of sources (triangulation).
- Use the results of data analysis for instructional purposes.

They also are positioned to *equip* other leaders throughout the district with the information and tools they need to enable more effective instruction. Useful strategies are listed below:

- Provide school leaders with the research knowledge and skills to intelligently disaggregate data and use it to drive instruction.
- Encourage a shared-governance style of leadership.
- Cultivate positive, caring relationships and consistently demonstrate servant leadership (become involved).
- Establish common learning language among everyone involved in the educational process to ensure a shared understanding of wording.
- Provide ongoing leadership training development, such as training in Mid-continent Research for Education and Learning's (McREL; 2003) 21 leadership competencies.

What Highly Effective
Principals and School Administrators Do

At the school level, these leaders also have *prioritizing* tasks, which are shown next:

- Recognize that teaching and learning are the top priority and demonstrate this by creating a rigorous and comprehensive curricular program, maximizing instructional time, making daily classroom visits, providing specific feedback (notes), and following up on classroom observations.
- Set the school's tone by communicating and implementing the school vision and/or mission effectively, persistently, and clearly.
- Hire high-quality, effective teachers and set clear expectations for high-quality teaching.

The best principals and school administrators support *learning* for everyone involved in the school, including themselves. They improve as leaders when they

- Develop "leader of leaders" skills, which include being a coach, partner, and cheerleader
- Master the science of data-driven instruction
- Grow as instructional leaders and understand how to apply instructional methods to promote student learning

Leading by example is a great way to emphasize the importance of instructional leadership. Administrators *model* instructional leadership when they

- Lead teachers in data discussions about student achievement and show them how to use the data to drive classroom instruction
- Model creative, research-based, learning-centered pedagogical strategies and monitor the implementation of these strategies and their impact on student learning
- Demonstrate situational, adaptive leadership but mainly supportive, participatory leadership (coming alongside teachers)

Principals and administrators can *build* supports in their schools to boost the effectiveness of each teacher. They must provide these supports:

- Serve constituents (especially teachers) by building positive relationships and open communication, resourcing their needs, and including them in the decision-making process.
- Enlarge the instructional leadership capacity of staff through an emphasis on staff development and empowerment.
- Provide workshops for teachers to hone their instructional skills.
- Galvanize the support of parents through engagement in the learning process.
- Establish professional learning communities with shared values that focus on monitoring data and improving student achievement.
- Champion the use of technologies that effectively support student learning.

Frontline Perspective

I utilize my key teacher leaders and administrators in delegating instructional criteria.

—High school principal

Frontline Perspective

You have to participate and become a part of the classroom instruction by modeling for teachers and providing meaningful professional development.

—District math coach

Frontline Perspective

Instructional Leadership models what's expected, it guides by involvement, and scaffolds to independence.

—High school exceptional student education teacher

- Hold classroom management at a premium and provide supportive training for teachers.

As more "localized" overseers of data, school leaders *analyze* data and guide staff in their analysis. They

Frontline Perspective

[I would tell administrators] to focus on instruction by encouraging their teachers to make instruction relevant and meaningful for the students.

—Middle school principal

- Enable teachers and staff to analyze data and focus on data-driven decision-making to drive classroom instruction and remediation
- Meet regularly with teachers to discuss and disaggregate data

Finally, as supervisors, school leaders are also tasked with *evaluating* their staff to ensure that effective instruction is being practiced, supported, and prioritized. Principals and administers should closely monitor teacher instruction and develop accountability tools for tracking and monitoring student progress.

What Highly Effective Teachers Do

The classroom is a source of the most data and the setting most responsive to action based on data analysis. Thus, *disaggregating* data is a major task for teachers. They

- Collect, analyze, and use data to identify goals
- Formulate strategic plans to achieve goals
- Constantly analyze data and use the results of data analysis for instructional purposes
- Track data analysis

Teachers also must *evaluate* the effectiveness or their instruction. They

Frontline Perspective

Leadership is a matter of being a genuine guide as well as being willing to be taught. Leadership is the love language of success.

—Elementary school music teacher

- Align the curriculum with state standards and instructional approaches with the curriculum
- Assess the impact of instruction and make adjustments in the instructional program

Just as school leaders must consider their own learning as part of the broad effort of the school, teachers must also *grow*. They build their knowledge and skills when they

- Refuse to accept failure as an option
- Visit the classrooms of highly effective peers

- Grow professionally through receiving in-service training, reading, subscribing to education journals, and obtaining advanced degrees
- Attend workshops to learn how to effectively use data to drive instruction

Finally, for their fellow teachers, their students, and the community at large, teachers themselves must *model* instructional leadership. Two ways to do this follow:

- Model servant leadership to students by caring for all students and meeting their needs. Use balanced pedagogical approaches with the emphasis on research-based, learning-centered approaches.
- Incorporate the seven correlates in their classrooms along with other best practices.

Supportive Research

Blanchard and Hodges (2005) describe leadership as "a process of influence" (p. 4). This process is evident at all levels of education, from the federal government to state, district, school, and classroom levels. However, the primary focus in this research discussion is on the instructional leadership of the school principal, because the influence of the principal affects the school—for better or for worse (McREL, 2003). *Instructional leadership* is therefore the principal's leadership influence that is brought to bear on instructional practices to promote student learning. Effective instructional leadership practices positively affect student learning, whereas ineffective practices have the obverse effect.

Principals Are Key to Effective Instructional Leadership Fullan (2001) stated, "The single most important factor ensuring that all students meet performance goals at the site level is the leadership of the principal—*leadership* being defined as 'the guidance and direction of instructional improvement'" (p. 126). Marzano (2003) stated, "Leadership may be considered the single most important aspect of effective school reform" (p. 172) and held that leadership undergirds all other factors (correlates) of effective schools. According to the Interstate School Leaders Licensure Consortium (ISLLC; Council of Chief State School Officers [CCSSO], 2008), effective educational leadership is key to the success of all tomorrow's students. Norton (2003) validates this assertion by holding that principals are the key to a school's climate and student learning. Peterson and Skiba (2001) share Norton's notion and view the role of the principal as crucial in determining the climate and success of the school. In essence, research studies suggest a correlation between the effective school principal's leadership and student achievement.

One example of the relationship between a principal's leadership and student academic achievement is clearly demonstrated by education researchers Waters, Marzano, and McNulty (2003). They conducted a meta-analysis under the auspices of McREL to examine the effects of leadership practices on student achievement. They conducted an exhaustive review of the literature and identified the following 21 key leadership responsibilities: culture; order; discipline; resources; curriculum, instruction, and assessment; focus; knowledge of curriculum and instruction assessment; visibility; contingent rewards; communication; outreach; input; affirmation; relationship; change agent; optimizer; ideals/beliefs; monitors/evaluates; flexibility; situational awareness; and intellectual stimulation.

The results clearly indicated "a substantial relationship between leadership (including instructional leadership) and student achievement" (Waters, Marzano, & McNulty, 2003, p. 3). The average effect size between leadership and student achievement was .25. If an average principal at an average school improves his or her abilities (in all 21 key leadership responsibilities identified by McREL) by one standard deviation, this translates into a 10% increase in mean student achievement—for example, an increase from the 50th percentile to the 60th percentile.

Other supportive studies by Grissom and Loeb (2009), Marks and Printy (2003), Cotton (2003), Van de Grift and Houtveen (1999), Bamburg and Andrews (1991), Hallinger, Bickman, and Davis (1996), and Winn, Erwin, Gentry, and Cauble (2009) also point to principals as being the keys to effective instructional leadership.

Gray (2009) notes the change in principals' responsibilities resulting from the NCLB era. "NCLB principals have a new set of responsibilities: disaggregating data, meeting with teachers about student learning, and providing leadership to create a professional learning community" (p. 2). Indeed, the Reading First Notebook (2005) argues, "Teaching and learning must be at the top of the [principal's] priority list on a consistent basis" (p. 1).

Prioritizing Instructional Leadership   The Interstate School Leaders Licensure Consortium (CCSSO, 2008) plays a pivotal role in enabling principals to be effective instructional leaders. It has identified six educational leadership standards that represent the broad, high-priority themes that education leaders must address in order to promote the success of every student. These six standards and their functions are noted in Table 8.1.

Although each of the six standards impinges on instructional leadership, the first two standards, in particular, assist principals in their quest to become highly effective instructional leaders.

Standard 1 states that "an education leader promotes the success of every student by facilitating the development, articulation, implementa-

Table 8.1. The Interstate School Leaders Licensure Consortium's 2008 educational leadership policy standards, as adopted by the National Policy Board for Educational Administration

Standard definition (An education leader promotes the success of every student by...)	Function
1. Facilitating the development, articulation, implementation, and stewardship of a vision of learning that is shared and supported by all stakeholders	A. Collaboratively develop and implement a shared vision and mission B. Collect and use data to identify goals, assess organizational effectiveness, and promote organizational learning C. Create and implement plans to achieve goals D. Promote continuous and sustainable improvement E. Monitor and evaluate progress and revise plans
2. Advocating, nurturing, and sustaining a school culture and instructional program conducive to student learning and staff professional growth	A. Nurture and sustain a culture of collaboration, trust, learning, and high expectations B. Create a comprehensive, rigorous, and coherent curricular program C. Create a personalized and motivating learning environment for students D. Supervise instruction E. Develop assessment and accountability systems to monitor student progress F. Develop the instructional and leadership capacity of staff G. Maximize time spent on quality instruction H. Promote the use of the most effective and appropriate technologies to support teaching and learning I. Monitor and evaluate the impact of the instructional program
3. Ensuring management of the organization, operation, and resources for a safe, efficient, and effective learning environment	A. Monitor and evaluate the management and operational systems B. Obtain, allocate, align, and efficiently utilize human, fiscal, and technological resources C. Promote and protect the welfare and safety of students and staff D. Develop the capacity for distributed leadership E. Ensure teacher and organizational time is focused to support quality instruction and student learning
4. Collaborating with faculty and community members, responding to diverse community interests and needs, and mobilizing community resources	A. Collect and analyze data and information pertinent to the educational environment B. Promote understanding, appreciation, and use of the community's diverse cultural, social, and intellectual resources C. Build and sustain positive relationships with families and caregivers D. Build and sustain productive relationships with community partners

(continued)

Table 8.1. *(continued)*

Standard definition *(An education leader promotes the success of every student by...)*	Function
5. Acting with integrity, fairness, and in an ethical manner	A. Ensure a system of accountability for every student's academic and social success
	B. Model principles of self-awareness, reflective practice, transparency, and ethical behavior
	C. Safeguard the values of democracy, equity, and diversity
	D. Consider and evaluate the potential moral and legal consequences of decision making
	E. Promote social justice and ensure that individual student needs inform all aspects of schooling
6. Understanding, responding to, and influencing the political, social, economic, legal, and cultural context	A. Advocate for children, families, and caregivers
	B. Act to influence local, district, state, and national decisions affecting student learning
	C. Assess, analyze, and anticipate

The Interstate School Leaders Licensure Consortium (ISLLC) Standards were developed by the Council of Chief State School Officers (CCSSO) and member states. Copies may be downloaded from the Council's website at www.ccsso.org.

From Council of Chief State School Officers. (2008). *Interstate School Leaders Licensure Consortium (ISLLC) standards for school leaders.* Washington, DC: Author; used by permission.

tion, and stewardship of a vision of learning that is shared and supported by all stakeholders" (CCSSO, 2008, p. 6). Consequently, there should be a collaborative development and implementation of the shared vision. The principal should lead the way in collecting and using data to identify goals, monitor institutional effectiveness, and promote learning. He or she must formulate strategic plans to achieve goals, foster ongoing school improvement, and revise plans based on monitoring and evaluation (CCSSO, 2008).

Standard 2 states that "an education leader promotes the success of every student by advocating, nurturing, and sustaining a school culture and instructional program conducive to student learning and staff professional growth" (CCSSO, 2008, p. 6).

Instructional leaders establish and sustain a culture that is conducive to learning by fostering and establishing collaboration, trust, and high expectations. They purposefully create a rigorous and comprehensive curricular program and establish a personalized learning environment that motivates students. Instructional leaders closely monitor teacher instruction and develop accountability tools for tracking and monitoring student progress. Enlarging the instructional capacity of staff is a pri-

Frontline Perspective

My instructional leadership style is leading by doing . . . and making myself available in case they need assistance.

—Elementary school teacher

ority, hence an emphasis on staff development. Instructional leaders seek to maximize the time spent on quality instruction and champion the use of technologies that effectively support student learning. They also assess the impact of instruction and make adjustments in the instructional program.

Motivation to Support Others There is a demonstrated link between instructional leadership and student academic achievement. Conversely, the lack of instructional leadership can result in educational disasters of titanic proportions. The key to effective instructional leadership is the heart motivation of the leader—that is, showing others that one genuinely cares about them as individuals. Greenleaf (2002) would agree that "washing the feet" of others, attending to their needs, and seeking the welfare of others first is the focus of the truly effective leader. Contained in this simple act of servant leadership are the keys to solutions that maximize the potential of students and improve academic achievement.

Frontline Perspective

I am a participative leader in all aspects. I know that if I show my students that I can do what I ask them to do, they will try to emulate my example. . . . I always perform the task . . . before they do it.

—Elementary school teacher

Effective instructional leaders are experts in pedagogical practices and demonstrate these to their staff and students. The question is, which pedagogical practices does one model? It seems that an age-old debate rages over camps of pedagogical practices, each complete with an arsenal of research to back up the particular camp's viewpoint.

I [Martin Ratcliffe] was raised in a British type of educational system in Rhodesia (now Zimbabwe), Africa. Content knowledge was high on the list, and teachers at the secondary levels in particular used mainly lecture-type delivery methods. I became quite adept at making copious notes and studying hard for exams. I then entered a teachers' college and was schooled in the latest pedagogical approaches of experiential, hands-on discovery, including the interdisciplinary integration of subjects. My training in the mid-1970s followed in the wake of the influential Plowden Report by the Central Advisory Council for Education (1967) in England. (The report praised child-centered approaches to education.) I entered public school teaching in Zimbabwe and then became an elementary school principal.

When I arrived in private education in the United States in the mid-1980s, I was shocked to see the retention of traditional approaches to education based on knowledge acquisition. Discovery, experiential-type learning was not the norm. Classes were structured, the curriculum was scripted—and students' academic scores were well ahead of their public school counterparts. Years later, upon my return to public school teaching, this time in American education, I was equally shocked to see the waning influence on co-

operative learning as NCLB quickly penetrated the echelons of public school education. All students had to make AYP, and I saw principals and teachers scramble back to the more traditional methods of teaching.

It seems as though the pendulum keeps swinging between two extreme pedagogical camps—the traditional "pouring in" (subject-centered) approach and the more creative, child-centered "drawing-out" or discovery camp. "Pouring-in" supporters such as direct instruction founder Engelmann (2007) and Chall (2000) share the belief that direct, teacher-centered instruction positively impacts student achievement. "Drawing-out" supporters such as Tsay and Brady (2010) and Brown and Ciuffetelli Parker (2009) also find a correlation between student-centered approaches and academic achievement. The research from both pedagogical camps and my own experience would suggest that these approaches are not mutually exclusive; to the contrary, effective instructional leaders have a broad repertoire of approaches to draw from, depending on the needs of the students, the subject matter at hand, the age of the learners, and class composition, among other factors.

After listening to a seminar on critical thinking by Dr. Velmarie Albertini, a behavioral science expert, I no longer have both feet in just one camp or even just one foot in both. Rather, I embrace a learning-centered approach, where I hold myself accountable for student learning and use research-based pedagogical approaches that will promote learning for every student.

SUMMARY

School principals are the single most important aspect of effective schooling (Marzano, 2003). The principal's failure to properly execute effective instructional leadership can therefore have potentially enormous repercussions. Or, as Maxwell (1998) puts it, "everything rises and falls on leadership" (p. 225).

The chapter's opening quote reminds us that "Involvement in Curriculum, Instruction, and Assessment is considered critical to the concept of instructional leadership" (Marzano, Waters, & McNulty, 2005, p. 53). Instructional leaders are adept at disaggregating the data and know how to guide teachers in effectively using the data to drive instruction. They hold student learning as their number one priority and communicate this school mission deliberately in every practice and policy.

Instructional leaders are hands-on when it comes to helping teachers to master effective pedagogical strategies. They personally model effective instructional practices for teachers and facilitate workshops to further equip teachers with effective, research-based instructional practices. They believe in improving their own instructional leadership skills and encourage teachers to do the same. Instructional leaders demonstrate servant leadership and go out of their way to ensure that teachers have the resources they need to be successful instructional leaders in the classroom. They encourage a shared mission and vision among all constituents, including parents. Effective instructional leaders are the key to the operationalization of the Instructional Leadership correlate and directly affect student academic success, helping schools to make the grade.

CASE STUDIES
SCHOOLS 1 AND 2

In looking at the track records of both Pine Grove Elementary and John D. Floyd K-8 Environmental Science School, it is obvious that the Instructional Leadership correlate was demonstrated by both administrators and staff. Both administrators agreed that they were the instructional leaders in their building, and they felt it was their duty to build leadership capacity throughout the school to support student growth and achievement.

Dave Dannemiller, former principal at Pine Grove, said that he considers himself a servant leader because he is always looking for ways to help teachers help students. "I am always asking the question, 'What can I do for you?'" he said. This was demonstrated in the data meetings he had with his teachers. He said that after discussing what strategies could be used to help raise a student's scores on an assessment, he would ask the teacher which resources he or she needed, whether additional time was needed for the student to reach a certain skill level, and how could he help to ensure that the student reached his or her goal. Dannemiller said he empowered teachers, team leaders, and parents to take ownership for the school and for the students so that everyone had a collective purpose. He said, "I set high expectations. I do a lot of collaboration. I am up front, honest, and very supportive."

Dannemiller emphasized that in addition to being a servant leader, he also had to be a situational leader, because there were times when he had to tell teachers what he wanted and how he wanted it done. An example of this was his requirement for teachers to keep a folder on students, especially struggling learners, that charted their growth. He said the required folder was used to generate discussions with teachers and teams on how to change instructional strategies in order to meet the students' needs. Dannemiller said he knew that as the instructional leader in his building, he had to continue to motivate teachers, support them, lead them in discussions about student achievement, and make sure that they implemented the strategies needed to ensure that students learned.

This can also be said of the former principal of John D. Floyd. Dr. Marcia Austin had required data meetings with teachers. She, like Dannemiller, monitored student progress and knew which students needed extra support in the classroom. She modeled for teachers and team leaders her expectations and made sure that everyone in the school was working toward the same mission. She said,

> As the instructional leader in the building, it was important that I exhibit a clear sense of direction in order to assist the teachers in prioritizing and focusing their attention on the things that mattered most, students and the curriculum. The dynamics within the building required that I practice adaptive leadership. Depending on the situation, I would fluctuate between being an authoritative, participatory, or delegative leader. But for the most part, I believe I exhibited a participatory-type leadership style.

Examples of Austin's instructional leadership were the required professional learning communities she held monthly with her team leaders, resource teachers, and assistant principals. She made sure that everyone was focused on student achievement, building a culture of shared learning and collaboration, and monitoring the data. Like Dannemiller, she had discussions with teachers on classroom pedagogy and individual student learning styles. She required teachers to attend workshops to learn instructional strategies that would help the students. In addition, she required each academic area and each grade level to set quarterly goals, which were monitored and reviewed.

More important, both Dannemiller and Austin were, and still are, approachable. They had open-door policies and welcomed teacher questions about student achievement, classroom instruction, and curriculum. In addition, both Dannemiller and Austin are passionate about students and education, which is evident in their words and actions. It is also evident in the stellar results they both led their former schools to accomplish.

However, it is important to note the difference in their leadership styles that may account for one school (Pine Grove) making AYP and not the other. Dannemiller points out that he used his leadership to create effective parent outreach programs and emphasized the need for parents to volunteer at Pine Grove Elementary School. As Lezotte and McKee (2002) state, in an effective school, "the principal acts as an instructional leader and effectively persistently communicates the mission of the school to staff, parents, and students" (p. 16). One of Dannemiller's strengths in leadership was his ability to galvanize parents and include them in the learning process. He ensured that they volunteered and took ownership of the school, provided them with different opportunities to get involved and learn strategies that could help their children at home, and provided learning workshops where they could ask questions and become more informed about the curriculum requirements. This presented a continuum that stemmed from the student and included the school as well as the parent in the child's education.

Although Austin communicated the school's mission and offered parents information about their children's learning, she admits that there was room for growth in this area. She could have used her leadership to strengthen that continuum, which would have had lasting results in the communication between the school and home; fostered partnerships in student learning; and provided more parent volunteering, which could have helped with remediation and enrichment services.

CHAPTER REFLECTION

1. Discuss your response to the chapter prompt: "Involvement in Curriculum, Instruction, and Assessment is considered critical to the concept of instructional leadership" (Marzano, Waters, & McNulty, 2005, p. 53). Give an example of a principal you know who demonstrates this involvement. What impact does he or she have on 1) teacher effectiveness, and 2) student achievement?

2. Compare and contrast instructional leadership strategies in a proficient and advanced school. What correlate strategies could a principal employ to make the transition from a proficient school to an advanced school? How? Give several examples.

3. How would you describe the instructional leadership role of a highly effective superintendent? Why is this leadership critical to student achievement? Give two or three research-supported reasons.

4. List three or four research sources that stress the critical impact that principals can have on student achievement. How can principals affect student achievement? Give two or three examples.

5. Identify the top three to five strategies that you believe highly effective principals use. Explain why you chose them and what they look like in practice.

6. Pick your favorite Frontline Strategy and explain why it is your favorite.

7. List several key strategies mentioned in the text that you could use to boost the presence of the Instructional Leadership correlate in your school district, school, or classroom. Why did you choose them? How would you implement them? How would you assess their effectiveness?

Safe and Orderly Environment Correlate

with James Dwight Davidson
and Heather Croft Jackson

The learning environment must be psychologically as well as physically safe for all students and must provide students with "safe havens in which to learn."

—M.L. Manning and K.T. Bucher (2003, p. 163)

Correlate Definition   In the effective school, we say there is an orderly, purposeful, business-like atmosphere which is free from the threat of physical harm. The school climate is not oppressive and is conducive to teaching and learning. (Lezotte & McKee, 2002, p. 17)

When I [James Dwight Davidson] moved to the Hugo School District in Oklahoma, I found schools in need of strong leadership to address myriad problems that included academic decline, a shifting student population, financial woes, and safety issues for starters. I recruited the help of an effective schools consultant, Dr. Steffens, who completed a comprehensive audit and introduced the district to the seven correlates of effective schools. Over the next 3 years, we experienced amazing success as we filtered the operation of the schools through all seven correlates. For example, yearly testing scores rose from 690 the first year to 1172 at the end of the third year (the state average was set at 1000). There was also a significant increase in safety.

When the opportunity to file for a Safe Schools and Healthy Students grant became available we leaped at the mere chance we might be so fortunate. Blessings rained on us, as we were a successful applicant. These monies assisted in two immediate ways. First, we were able to modify some of our personnel without having massive layoffs. This was quite necessary so that people could be moved to key positions which required certain skills and strengths which were necessary for implementation of various rules, regulations and requirements of both students and staff. Second, this afforded us an extension of time to rectify the financial balance until we could change the actual nature as well as the community's perception of the school district and its environment.

Preliminary survey information obtained prior to the grant submittal indicated over 70% of the respondents (students, faculty, staff, parents, and community) were quite concerned about the perceived lack of a safe and orderly environment existing (particularly at the high school level). With the statistical information as well as the theoretical support, we could now start the process of closely determining just what was going on and what could be done about such a situation both short and long term. Plans were made, adjustments were discussed and determined for all sites, and steps of implementation were initiated.

Amazingly, within 6 months of actual implementation, survey results indicated the fear factor of an Unsafe and Disorderly environment had shrunk dramatically. This issue dropped from #1 ranking of school wide concerns to #18 overall. Likewise, it went from over 70% of the respondents noting their concern to the perceived problem to less than 10% even noting it of any fashion at all. This spectacular shift in opinion was attributed to a number of steps taken: first, the simple act of straightforwardly assessing the safety and behavioral issues at hand and not soft-pedaling the impact they were having on the school; second, addressing the issues with appropriate force; and third, clearly communicating and telling the story to any and all shareholders so that they were all on the same page and united in their sense of urgency as well as in their ability to recognize the successes as they mounted. Cumulatively the effect

Frontline Perspective

Students must feel safe before teachers can provide effective instruction.

—District math coach

was to change the entire perception and actual nature of the school district's engagement with the students and their behavior patterns.

One of the early changes was to shift the high school from a block schedule format to a 7 period day. Our rationale was that too much time was being wasted. The students had a protest and walked out of class (calling the area television news outlets), the teachers (approximately one half of the high school) actively sought to discredit the change, and we stood in our resolve that this was a very important step in reclaiming our high school's environment and sending a message: there was a new sheriff in town and the times they were a-changin'. Interestingly, some of the protesting students took their banners and signs to Main Street to get more attention to their plight. They were met with indifference and soon decided this was not fun. We did not punish them for not attending class (later in the year we added a day for attendance purposes). My one interaction with them as superin-

tendent was to approach them, as they eased out on the road, and request/ implore them to please get back on the sidewalk for their own safety—noting to them at the time, this whole issue was an attempt to deal with their safety which they themselves had told us was paramount to them (via their survey information). Instead of scorn or derision they kindly thanked me for caring and in about 5 minutes disbanded and drifted back to school (about three blocks from where they were).

This seemed to be a critical turning point, which had been planned and orchestrated using the correlate of a Safe and Orderly Environment as a key component of argument and support to our developing posture and positioning. The local newspaper gave a fair account of the situation and sought and received an inside understanding of the true issues at hand. It became an impartial yet intricate part of our communication efforts to the community on this and other issues or endeavors.

Inappropriate behavior at the high school was addressed on the first day of school. The new principal, a man of few words (but loud actions), welcomed the students in a general assembly in the gym and noted their expected behavior would be reflected by the rules and regulations of their handbook, which was virtually the same as the previous years, and that they would be expected to adhere to said rules.

Immediately one individual challenged the principal with a defiant remark. The principal calmly reiterated the rules would be adhered to this year regardless of what might have existed in the past. At this time the principal also instructed the young man to please exit from the back to have his trousers properly adjusted (they were sagging) prior to returning to the assembly. This was accomplished, and henceforth the student body became aware that a Safe and Orderly Environment would be maintained and done so fairly and consistently, regardless of whom the offender might be or believe themselves to be. Soon this posturing led to additional potential problems cropping up that required equally engaging efforts on the principal's part in order to still the waters of discontent.

THE IMPORTANCE OF A SAFE AND ORDERLY ENVIRONMENT

Developing a safe and orderly school environment is vital for academic achievement. According to Maslow's hierarchy of needs, students cannot perform academically until all of their basic physical, safety, love, and self-esteem needs are met, respectively (Ormrod, 2009). Meichenbaum (n.d.) states that "between 20% and 50% of American children are victims of violence within their families, at school, or in their communities. Such victimization experiences contribute to impaired school functioning, decreased IQ and reading ability, lower grade point average, more days of school absence and decreased rates of high school graduation" (p. 5). Further, behavioral disorders and emotional deficits are directly linked to "aggressive and delinquent behavior" as well as "Post Traumatic Stress Disorder, anxiety, and depression disorders" (Meichenbaum, n.d., p. 5).

Neurobiologically speaking, children who experience trauma and compromised safety may experience altered brain growth (Meichenbaum, n.d.). Altered brain growth affects the brain's ability to communicate among functional structures of the brain for storage and retrieval of information due to functional and structural changes within itself. Brains of students with trauma experiences have decreased brain synaptic connections, making communication between parts of the brain very difficult (Leaf, 2008). Decreased brain synaptic connections are like telephone poles with missing or dysfunctional telephone lines that impede communication. Students who experience compromised safety in their schools and community will suffer physically, emotionally, socially, and cognitively, which directly influences academic performance.

Finally, Meichenbaum (n.d.) notes that children who experience trauma, especially abuse, "are seven times more likely to show evidence of left hemisphere deficits. This can contribute to the failure to develop self-regulatory functions, especially language and memory abilities" (p. 10). Students who have left-hemispheric brain malfunction "show deficits in attention and abstract reasoning/executive functions, and experience short-term memory deficits" (Meichenbaum, n.d., p. 12). Hannaford (2005) summarizes the impact of safe and threatening learning environments:

> CAT [computerized axial tomography] scans show that children process information through their emotions first, and information that is most emotional and emotionally relevant to them, is what students will learn. On the other hand, insecurity and fear can bring learning to a screeching halt by shutting down higher brain connections. (p. 62)

It is imperative that school be conducted in an orderly manner, with school and classroom management policies clearly spelled out and consistently enforced. Classroom management professor and former assistant school principal, Dr. Leonard Giammatteo (personal communication, January 11, 2011) stresses that an orderly school environment is necessary because it 1) promotes a physically and emotionally safe learning environment, 2) creates structure, 3) provides an atmosphere that promotes learning and achievement, and 4) enables students to feel comfortable and learn better in the absence of undue anxiety. Giammatteo stresses that an orderly environment begins with the school leadership and involves all constituents. He points out that teachers can ensure an orderly learning environment by managing their classrooms well. In particular, teachers should 1) build a learning community, 2) consistently implement a discipline plan across the board, 3) have clear teaching procedures and routines, 4) build social skills, and 5) build the affective domain. Giammatteo urges parents to consistently reinforce the school expectations and procedures and attend teacher–parent conferences.

STRATEGIES FOR MAINTAINING
A SAFE AND ORDERLY ENVIRONMENT

Establishing a positive environment and developing safety plans requires collaboration among all stakeholders. The following strategies involve educators at all levels. The themes across these strategies include ensuring, securing, implementing, communicating, directing, building, establishing, creating, and enforcing.

What Highly Effective
Superintendents and District Administrators Do

Leaders at the district level *ensure* that plans are in place and good practices are supported in every school. Effective superintendents and district administrators use the strategies below:

- Perform a safety assessment such as Safe Schools Assessment and Resource Bank (SSARB; n.d.).
- Involve constituents and create a comprehensive, well-rehearsed, and widely communicated district and school safety plan.
- Promote the physical safety and cleanliness of buildings.
- Offer district trainings on the importance of a safe and orderly environment in schools.
- Provide each school with emergency schoolwide procedures and ensure that they are in place.
- Build community confidence through positive and proactive communication.

   Broad efforts for *security* at schools also fall under the responsibility of these high-level leaders as they do the following:

- Partner with school personnel, students, parents, and the community to establish safe schools.
- Obtain grants to help schools adopt programs such as the Safe Schools / Healthy Students Initiative (U.S. Department of Education, n.d.-b).
- Maximize the use of technology and use security cameras to help create a safe and orderly environment.
- Recruit the services of educational consultants who will provide an objective audit and strategic plan for improving school safety.
- Monitor and strategically operationalize the seven correlates.

Finally, these administrators broadly *implement* measures that promote safe and orderly environments when they

- Assess the safety and behavioral issues straightforwardly
- Address behavioral and safety issues with appropriate force
- Communicate the story to stakeholders

What Highly Effective
Principals and School Administrators Do

As liaisons between the district, the community, teachers, and students, school administrators *communicate* about safety. These leaders take these steps:

- Demonstrate that student safety on campus is the number one priority.
- Establish and consistently enforce clear and fair schoolwide school rules and procedures.
- Creatively broadcast the Safe and Orderly Environment correlate through a variety of social occasions.
- Post the school rules, rationale, rewards, and consequences.
- Use safety meetings to review emergency procedures.
- Involve constituents in problem solving with an emphasis on open and honest communication.
- Conduct parent feedback surveys.

Frontline Perspective

Our expectations are our driving force. We say them every morning along with our mission statement. Throughout the day, they are used as reminders for their behavior.

—Elementary school assistant principal

Frontline Perspective

I set clear expectations and consistently follow through with established rewards and consequences. Students know what to expect and can make informed decisions.

—High school principal

Principals and school administrators *direct* initiatives at the school level, which means they use these approaches:

- Build school programs that ensure a safe and orderly environment on campus by involving all constituents (teachers, staff, students, parents, and community).
- Enforce a systemic (schoolwide) behavioral management plan.
- Maintain strong leadership in dealing with students with aggressive behaviors and those who spread fear and intimidation.
- Initiate mentoring programs for troubled youth based on school needs.

Principals and school administrators also work on a more hands-on basis to implement the efforts to improve the school's environment. Highly effective school leaders do the following:

- Implement school, class, and individual scheduling changes to reduce "idle" time.
- Ensure the high visibility of the principal in classrooms and on campus.
- Establish mentoring programs for troubled youth.
- Encourage all adults, especially teachers, to accept that they are on duty continually and in every location (because the success of the Safe and Orderly Environment correlate depends on them).
- Create a positive school climate and learning environment for students by maintaining safe and attractive buildings and surroundings.
- Create student support teams.
- Create a schoolwide support team.

What Highly Effective Teachers Do

At the classroom level, teachers on a daily basis *build* trust and a feeling of safety when they take these steps:

- Foster positive teacher–student and student–student relationships by nurturing a spirit of connection and community and fostering a caring learning environment.
- Use humor.
- Use sincere language and engage in meaningful conversations with students.
- Solicit collaborative buy-in from students by allowing them some say in class-governance procedures.

As leaders within the classroom, teachers also *establish* expectations about the quality of the environment. Highly effective teachers use these strategies:

- Institute classroom procedures that promote a safe and orderly environment from the first day.
- Create a feeling of safety and security.

Frontline Perspective

Relationships will give students a reason for coming to school by making school a meaningful part of the student's life.

—Middle school principal

Frontline Perspective

The routines I establish beginning the first day...help keep our room orderly. . . . There are clear consequences when they're not followed.

—Elementary school teacher

- Model effective classroom management skills.
- Communicate high expectations for students to maintain a safe and orderly classroom environment.
- Take ownership of classroom behavior by enforcing the policies and procedures fairly, firmly, and consistently.

Teachers also support student safety by *creating* ways for students to learn about safety and modeling a good environment. Some strategies of this nature follow:

- Generate lessons on the importance of safety and orderly behavior in school.
- Facilitate a positive learning environment for students partly by maintaining an attractive, safe, orderly, and clean classroom.
- Implement positive behavior supports (PBS). According to Cohn, PBS "is an empirically validated, function-based approach to eliminate challenging behaviors and replace them with prosocial skills" and "decreases the need for more intrusive or aversive interventions (i.e., punishment or suspension) and can lead to both systemic as well as individualized change" (2001, p. 1).

Frontline Perspective

My room is neat and clean. . . . It serves me well for organization.

—High school teacher

Finally, as the closest supervisors of students, teachers are tasked with *enforcing* rules that promote student safety and orderliness of the school. Highly effective teachers actively do these things:

- Enforce procedures that eliminate chaos in halls, cafeteria, and playground.
- Follow the school's discipline referral procedures.
- Enforce a no-bullying policy.

I (Martin Ratcliffe) was a newly appointed school leader of a bustling pre-K-12th grade setting, which included an elementary, middle, and high school. Here are three events that very quickly prompted me to initiate a comprehensive schoolwide safety plan.

During my initiation and before assuming the official reins, I attended a kindergarten graduation. The program went well until the stage curtains started smoldering from a hot stage bulb. We quickly evacuated everybody and removed the smoldering curtain.

On day one, an irate and threatening parent stormed into my office demanding to know the whereabouts of his children. However, he was not the legal guardian and we could not help him. Several hours later he left my office somewhat calmer. The tact, prayer, and counseling had apparently taken effect.

> *A few days later, inclement weather struck and 15 tornadoes touched down in our county, one of them just a mile away from the school. We followed the rehearsed tornado drill and had everyone safely positioned in the hallways. A safe and orderly environment was my top priority.*

Supportive Research

Flanagain (2007) calls the question of safety among the most profound issues facing today's schools. Proficient schools emanate a nonoppressive atmosphere that is conducive to learning; they are purposeful and efficiently businesslike. They are also noted in terms of the absence of specific undesirable behaviors. Advanced schools have an increased emphasis on certain desirable behaviors such as teamwork. When teachers model cooperative teamwork and teach students to respect human diversity and appreciate democratic values, they can anticipate an advanced school where students emulate their teachers and help one another. The success of the Safe and Orderly Environment correlate depends on all adults, especially teachers, accepting that they are on duty continually and in every location (Lezotte, 1997; Lezotte & McKee, 2002). Taylor (2009) holds that school safety and security are paramount.

Frontline Perspective

At the beginning of the school year, we have a long discussion on safety and expectations in the classroom. . . . Throughout the year, these rules and expectations are discussed to make sure that the students don't forget.

—Middle school teacher

Teachers Are Key to Building a Safe and Orderly Environment

Building a positive environment that is conducive to learning is the quest of effective educators. According to the Center for Comprehensive School Reform and Improvement (2009), a positive school climate enhances the learning environment and is a win–win situation for teachers and students. Harry and Rosemary Wong (2009) have dedicated their lives to showing teachers how to build such a learning environment. They remind us that 1) "teacher preparation is the key for teacher success" (p. 12), 2) teachers should have positive expectations of their students, 3) clear procedures from day one are critical to effective classroom management, and 4) lesson mastery is vital to creating an engaging and meaningful environment that promotes student learning.

Frontline Perspective

I start with a skeletal blueprint of classroom rules and allow students to add their own. They take ownership of the rules, which promotes a positive, self-correcting atmosphere.

—High school teacher

How School Districts Assess School Safety   There are many established methods for school districts to use to assess their school safety needs and climate. One of those established methods of school safety assessments is the SSARB, a questionnaire that allows school districts to collect data relating to the strengths and weaknesses of their schools with safe school practices guidelines.

SSARB survey questions are based on 32 key school safety and climate factors, including academic engagement, cultural sensitivity, parent and community involvement, school communication, crisis preparedness, drug and alcohol usage, and bullying (Montana Safe Schools Center, n.d.).

School districts should use all stakeholders as participants in the assessment, including teachers, students, and parents. All participants complete the questionnaires online through a secure Internet server. Upon completion, the participants' scores are tallied and formulated into a password-authorized electronic report. Administrators may view the report data in graphic picture representations as well as narrative summaries. School districts also have the option of comparing their data to other anonymously stored district, state, and national data. Results are mapped across six topics: 1) community involvement, 2) discipline, 3) perceptions of safety, 4) school services, 5) staff preparedness, and 6) violence and victimization (Services, n.d.). "SSARB results are also linked to an electronic library with hundreds of evidence-based resources proven to help improve school safety—all linked to the specific issues presented from the school's survey results" (Montana Safe Schools Center, n.d., paragraph 6). These evidence-based resources help school districts create action plans for immediate implementation in their schools.

SSARB may be purchased through Sopris West Educational Services or purchased through grant funding. For example, in the state of Montana, SSARB is funded through grant funding and congressional backing; in fact, since the fall of 1998, over 60,000 students, staff, and parents have participated in the online assessment as a "requirement of schools participating in the Montana Office of Public Instruction's Montana Behavioral Initiative" (Montana Safe Schools Center, n.d., paragraph 2).

Involving the teachers, students, and parents in activities such as safety assessments can help build a sense of community within school districts; Jones and Jones (2010) noted that "students can build a sense of community by solving a common problem or sharing in assisting others . . . [as shown in] the classic Sherif experiment conducted in 1958" (p. 115).

Create a Student Support Team and a Schoolwide Support Team
Building a safe community begins with creating a team of people from the school district who understand principles of safe community school environments, developmental stages of child development, and behavioral man-

agement strategies. The first team to develop is the Student Support Team, which is sometimes known as the Child Study Team or the Student Assistance Team (Dwyer & Osher, 2000). This team develops first because the people on the Student Support Team are usually involved directly with the students in the schools on a one-to-one basis, such as classroom teachers, parents, special education teachers, students, and other agency providers.

The second team to develop is the Schoolwide Support Team. This group usually involves people from the school and the community, such as parents, students, community agencies, law enforcement officials, psychologists, health professionals, clergy, business leaders, and other stakeholders. Dwyer and Osher (2000) noted that "the Schoolwide Team is sometimes called the School Management Team or School Improvement Team. While the primary functions of these two teams [Student Support Team and Schoolwide Team] are different, both teams are necessary to create safe, educationally sound learning environments" (p. 5). A minimum of three key people—a principal, teacher, and mental health professional—should serve on both teams to assist in coordination and communication between the teams (Dwyer & Osher, 2000).

According to Dwyer and Osher, the Schoolwide Team should have expertise and credibility in the following seven areas:

- Prevention, early intervention, and intensive intervention
- School reform
- Community resources
- Family concerns
- Student concerns
- Staff concerns
- Administrative concerns (2000, p. 6)

The Schoolwide Team is responsible for conducting and reviewing safety needs assessments, developing a violence and crisis prevention plan for the school district with links to community support, and implementing and monitoring the violence and crisis prevention plan (Dwyer & Osher, 2000). The Schoolwide Team meets at designated times weekly or monthly and remains in close communication with liaisons from the Student Support Team to accomplish goals of formulating, establishing, and maintaining a safe psychological and physical school climate while supplying community support (Dwyer & Osher).

Addressing Inappropriate Behavior   Addressing inappropriate behaviors in the school environment can be challenging but is not impossible. There are many resources available to help school districts set up effective mentoring and behavior programs that address areas such as bullying, violence, social training, ethics, life skills training, early intervention, and ca-

reer development. Two resource Internet sites that may be beneficial starting points for schools districts are http://www.TeachSafeSchools.org and
http://www.apahelpcenter.org. (Meichenbaum, n.d.). Both sites have numerous listings to help any school dis-
trict leader find programs for implementation into their school district's safe
school plan. The National Association
of School Psychologists (2001) noted
that "schools implementing effective
strategies have reported reductions in
office discipline referrals by 20-60%;
this results in improved access to aca-
demic engaged time and improved academic performance for all students."

Establishing a Safe Community   School districts must partner with
school personnel, students, parents, and the community to establish safe
schools. A safe community is one that 1) promotes psychological and physical safety in school activities during regular school hours as well as during
after-school programs and 2) establishes crisis management plans or protocols to use in case of emergencies (Osher, Dwyer, & Jimerson, 2006). For
schools to remain vital and integral parts in communities, parents must
want their children to attend local schools. "Negative images of the school
can strongly affect a school's public image," thus affecting attendance rates
and public support (Center for Comprehensive School Reform and Improvement, 2009, p. 7).

Zero Tolerance Policies: Helpful or Harmful to School Safety?
Using zero tolerance policies in a school safety plan can actually harm
school image. As Peterson and Schoonover (2008) noted, "harsh consequences may have a negative effect on student perceptions of school climate, and may cause school administrators to be associated with actions not
in the interest of children or the community" (p. 2). Zero tolerance policies
promote the perception that the school has safety under control, when in
actuality they limit school personnel's ability to make sound judgments
about safety management. Peterson and Schoonover pointed out that

> The American Bar Association (2001) and a number of professional
> associations have adopted statements opposing the use of zero toler-
> ance policies in schools because they might limit the ability of admin-
> istrators to consider the circumstances or nature of the offense or
> the student's history (e.g. American Psychological Association, 2006).
> (2008, p. 1)

In fact, research has shown that zero tolerance policies do not reduce violence and do not improve student behaviors (Peterson & Schoonover, 2008).

One major concern expressed in the research appears to be the one-size-fits-all approach to punishment incurred for an infraction. It seems that common sense sometimes takes a back seat and potentially minor infractions escalate out of proportion. For example, Chen (2009) observed that

> Students who are unintentionally and often unknowingly breaking the rules are punished severely under the zero tolerance policy. Adding to this, the zero tolerance rules do not acknowledge individual students' emotional, intellectual, or learning disabilities. Oftentimes, misbehavior cases involving students with disabilities arise from their own personal challenges—and not due to their intent to cause harm or malice towards others. (2009, p. 1)

Chen hastened to acknowledge, however, that "despite the criticism of zero tolerance rules, according to data from the United States Justice Policy Institute and the Department of Education, crime and violence have decreased by 30 percent in all public schools since 1990" (2009, p. 2).

Positive Behavior Supports and Safety According to Amy Bratten, ESOL Education Professor,

> Positive Behavior Support (PBS) is a school-wide discipline program that is implemented to focus on rewarding acceptable behavior as opposed to punishing negative behavior. It lists expectations instead of rules. If a student does not live up to the expectations, instead of punishment, the classroom teacher discusses the infraction with the student and assists the student in developing a plan for modeling acceptable behavior in the future. (A. Bratten, personal communication, January 11, 2011)

PBS (instead of zero tolerance policies) has shown promising effectiveness in student behavior, violence prevention, and discipline reduction (Peterson & Schoonover, 2008). Cohn (2001) stated, "PBS can target an individual student or an entire school, as it does not focus exclusively on the student, but also includes changing environmental variables such as the physical setting, task demands, curriculum, instructional pace and individualized reinforcement" (para. 2). In fact, Cohn (2001) stated, "research on PBS effectiveness showed that there was over a 90% reduction in problem behavior in over half of the studies; the problem behavior stopped completely in over 26% of the studies" (para. 11). PBS helps increase prosocial behavior and increase on-task student behavior, which directly affects academic performance (Cohn).

Technology and Safety Another way to improve the public image of a safe school is to incorporate technology into the school safety plan. The use of technology to ensure safety could prove useful for all schools due to its speed of safety checks for school entry, especially with those schools with histories of violence. Uchida, Maguire, Solomon, and Gantley (2004) recommend using iris recognition technology for staff, student, parent, and visitor school entry along with video surveillance cameras throughout the campus as well as video camera monitors and conventional buzzers at entry sites. Uchida et al. reported no negative perceptions of safety by parents using the devices and reported that parents liked the speed of the scan versus the old policy of identity verification. Plus, Uchida et al. reported an increased perception of safety by teachers within the school.

Many schools also use video monitoring on their school buses. According to the National Law Enforcement and Corrections Technology Center, "Technology can now produce checklists of students who have boarded buses and instantly transmit those checklists back to school offices. Technologies that track the locations of buses and trains for public transit systems also can be applied to school buses" (2003, p. 2). Schools use metal detector scanners like those found in airports to increase student safety and prevent gun and knife entries onto student campuses.

Schools often have limited resources for assessing technologies and deciding on their use in comprehensive safety plans. Schools may have varying needs based on their background and community context when it comes to incorporating technologies. However, one thing is certain, and that is that all schools must secure a safe and orderly environment to help maximize learning for all students. For schools that would like to use technology in their school safety plans, one organization to contact is the National Institute of Justice (NIJ), which sponsors a program called the School Safety Program (National Law Enforcement and Corrections Technology Center, 2003). NIJ helps schools evaluate safety technology and incorporate technology into their safety measures. For more information on NIJ School Safety Program initiatives, visit their web site at http://www.ojp .usdoj.gov/nij/sciencetech/sst.htm.

SUMMARY

The chapter's opening quote reminds us that "the learning environment must be psychologically as well as physically safe for all students and must provide students with 'safe havens in which to learn'" (Manning & Bucher, 2003, p.163). Students who experience unsafe conditions of stress and trauma can experience states of arrested development in brain growth. This leads to decreased abilities in encoding, storing, and retrieval of information in cognitive learning brain structures, which directly affect reading abilities, attention, and self-regulation. An orderly and safe learning environment is therefore a prerequisite for student learning.

An effective school fosters a positive school climate through strong and purposeful leadership that proactively broadcasts the school safety rules and seeks collaborative buy-in from constituents. Such a school deals with misbehavior firmly and fairly. Lezotte and McKee (2002) stated that in an effective school, the school leadership creates "an orderly, purposeful, business-like atmosphere which is free from the threat of physical harm" (p. 17). Buildings are properly maintained and cleaned, classrooms are orderly, and teachers manage student behavior effectively by establishing classroom routines.

School districts that develop safe schools form Student Support Teams and Schoolwide Support Teams to conduct safety assessments, create safety plan designs, promote safety plan implementation, and perform safety evaluation measures. Safety plans must ensure the physical and psychological well-being of school district staff and students as well as provide for crisis management during emergency situations. Partnering with community organizations and leaders is crucial in building and supporting safe schools.

School safety plans and school administrative management practices must reflect good judgment to establish and maintain a positive public image. A positive public school image can be developed and sustained through PBS rather than zero tolerance policies and through the infusion of technology into school safety plans.

School districts that are committed to safe school policies believe in staff and student safety as well as student achievement. Safety and student achievement are directly linked. When teachers develop positive relationships with students, and when all school constituents work collaboratively under the leadership of the principal to create a safe and orderly environment and feeling of community, then there is no limit to the good that can be accomplished—and no limit to the increases in student academic achievement and schools that make the grade.

CASE STUDIES
SCHOOLS 1 AND 2

At Pine Grove Elementary, one example of the way teachers and administrators ensure there is a safe and orderly environment on the campus is to have the students walk one behind the other as they move along the pathways. Another is how students routinely line up in the cafeteria and get their lunch and then sit at their assigned table. Former principal Dave Dannemiller said this orderliness was important, because to create a safe and orderly environment the school must have an organized structure in place in which students knew the rules and expectations. "That was almost a necessity with having almost 1,400 students," he says. "We had a way students walked in line. Of course, we encouraged students to follow the procedures through positive reinforcement." Dannemiller explained that he supported a "Best Bears" program at his former school where students were rewarded for doing what was expected of them such as walking quietly in line down the school sidewalk and following the rules in the cafeteria. He said this program was built on the support of everyone in the school community. A teacher could give a student recognition or it could come from an office staff member who saw a student following school rules and procedures. In this way, Dannemiller stated, students learned to be responsible for their actions because everyone was watching their behavior.

Inside the classroom, students were expected to adhere to school procedures and expectations as well. Dannemiller said that he expected teachers to work with students behaviorally to let them and the other students know that the classroom was a safe and organized place to be. He said, "One thing that frustrates me is if a teacher is struggling with a student behaviorally or academically and they want administration to do something about the student. I always ask, 'What have you done to make sure that student feels safe in your classroom? What are your routines and procedures? What have you done to try to change the behaviors?' Calling a parent is a first step and an expectation, but it doesn't stop there. To create an orderly classroom environment, the teacher has to take ownership first and then I can support him or her. They can't just pass along their ownership and then acquiesce."

Similarly, walking down the corridor at John D. Floyd K-8 Environmental School, one can clearly see the blue lines that mark where the elementary students are supposed to walk in lines. From the time students enter kindergarten, they are taught how to walk down the corridor, how to line up in the cafeteria, and what route they are supposed to take from the bus to their classroom. This orderliness is pivotal, especially with middle school students also on the campus. Originally, the school had two start times and end times to maintain safety on the campus, with the elementary and middle school students both using main facilities such as the administration building, the media center, and the cafeteria. However, once the district decided to change the dual start and end times at the school for financial reasons, the administration had to ensure that middle school students knew the expectations when they walked on the campus, especially if elementary students were changing classes as well.

Therefore, the routines and expectations created an orderliness that caused students to feel safe on an open campus despite the 1,700 student population. "We made sure that schoolwide discipline procedures were in place," said Marcia Austin, former principal at John D. Floyd. "This involved posting the rules, explaining the rules, warning students, communicating with parents, consequences within the classroom, and if needed, an administrative referral to the office. Teachers were expected to develop positive relationships with the students and yet be in control of their class-room."

For the Safe and Orderly Environment correlate, both schools satis-fied Lezotte and McKee's (2002) definition of an effective school: "an or-derly, purposeful, business-like atmosphere which is free from the threat of physical harm. The school climate is not oppressive and is conducive to teaching and learning" (p. 17). Both maintained schoolwide systems for student behavior and instruction that promoted a safe environment for stu-dents. They both established and maintained clear and consistent routines to ensure that students were not placed in danger. In addition, communi-cation systems were in place to include all stakeholders in ensuring that stu-dents were safe and secure.

CHAPTER REFLECTION

1. Discuss your response to the chapter prompt, "The learning environ-ment must be psychologically as well as physically safe for all students and must provide students with 'safe havens in which to learn'" (Man-ning & Bucher, 2003, p.163). Give two or three examples showing the importance of the Safe and Orderly Environment correlate.

2. If you were a school principal, how would you establish a safe and or-derly learning environment? Give a scenario. Use examples from the chapter to help support your stance.

3. You are a new superintendent brought in to help turn around a strug-gling school district. List five to seven safety issues you might en-counter and how you would address each one. What would you rely on the most in addressing these issues?

4. Contrast a proficient and an advanced school in terms of establishing the Safe and Orderly Environment correlate. What practical steps would you take to establish the correlate at each level? At which level do you think the Hugo School District (mentioned in the chapter's open-ing example) was after the implementation of the correlates? Explain.

5. Identify the top three to five strategies mentioned in the text that you could use to boost the presence of this correlate in your school district, school, or classroom. Why did you choose them? How would you im-plement them? How would you assess their effectiveness?

6. According to the research, how might the absence of a safe and orderly environment adversely affect student learning? Give two or three spe-cific examples from the research.

7. Choose a school level (elementary, middle, or high) and design a school poster that positively promotes the Safe and Orderly Environment correlate to its constituents, especially students. Include five to seven key points that would remind students what to do and why.

The Clarion Call

Nothing creative happens until energy is forced into a discipline.

—W.J. Cook, Jr. (2000, p. 115)

The perceived student achievement crisis has racked up numerous studies that have convinced the U.S. Congress to take action and hold schools accountable for student academic growth. To achieve this goal, Congress reauthorized the ESEA (PL 89-10), the principal federal law affecting education from kindergarten through high school, with the passage of the landmark NCLB Act of 2001 (PL 107-110). This act requires every state to develop challenging standards for students and requires that all students achieve proficiency on state-defined education standards by the end of the 2013–2014 school year.

AYP scores are the accountability tool used by NCLB to determine whether all students are learning in the specified subgroups and whether the learning gap between the subgroups is closing. All federally funded schools are required to make AYP or else face severe penalties that range from identification as a failing school to complete restructuring. To date, it appears that America's schools are still in the grips of the student achievement crisis and need help making AYP. Secretary of Education Arne Duncan had this to say about benchmark National Assessment of Educational Progress results: "The achievement of American students isn't growing fast enough. . . . Students aren't making the progress necessary to compete in the global economy. . . . Our students aren't on a path to graduate high school ready to succeed in college and the workplace" (U.S. Department of Education, 2010b, p. 1).

CORRELATE SOLUTIONS

We, the authors, recognize the seriousness of the current time. We know that education in America is undergoing tectonic changes. We see daily evidences of the powerful NCLB federal legislation and how it is changing the course of business as usual and driving the massive educational ship. Furthermore, we are cognizant of the provisions in the Blueprint for Reform: The Reauthorization of the Elementary and Secondary Education Act proposed by the U.S. Department of Education, which promises yet additional education reforms.

We also recognize the challenges that educators face on a daily basis in trying to help students learn. We really do hear your almost audible groaning and even anguish as you give your all to meet the near-impossible demands of AYP. We want to thank you for your contribution and dedication to education, whether at the district administrative level, school level, or classroom level. You are making a difference in the lives of students. Education is more than a number on a piece of paper; it involves the whole student. Education is still the number one profession, as reported in surveys (Johnson, Musial, Hall, & Gollnick, 2011). We have been where you are, under the daily pressures of accountability, and we know that sometimes even good schools can be perceived as failing schools if they do not make AYP. (Such was the case in one of our case study comparison schools, John D. Floyd K-8 Environmental Science School, as detailed in Chapters 3–9.)

We have also done our homework. We have done the research, invited contributing experts to join us in this book, analyzed the data, conducted surveys, and listened to educators on the front lines. And we have good news to share with you: All is not lost. It is possible to increase student learning and to see it sustained over time. Students can make AYP—and they can make it in successive years. Certainly, it takes a lot of hard work. Effective teachers do work hard. But it also takes smart work. That means looking to what the research has said really works over the long haul. This means examining the characteristics of effective and highly effective schools that have been identified in multiple studies over time, and believing in our students.

Effective schools researchers from the early 1970s to the present time showed that schools do make a difference. This is a contrary claim to that made in Coleman et al. (1966) and corroborating studies. These researchers claimed that schools make little difference and that home environment and socioeconomic factors are the determinants of student academic success. Effective schools researchers show that effective schools have a strong presence of the correlates, whereas ineffective schools do not. In addition, correlate studies link the correlates to student achievement scores. Furthermore, the AYP–correlate study demonstrates a significant relationship between the correlates and AYP scores (Ratcliffe, 2006). The way to work smarter and to see sustained increases in student learning and student achievement scores where schools *make the grade* is to purposefully cultivate a strong presence of the correlates in schools. Both case study schools were successful in making an "A" grade from the state; however, Pine Grove was particularly successful as indicated by the school making AYP.

CASE STUDY
EPILOGUE

The two case study schools visited in Chapters 3–9 were sister schools located 10 miles apart. Pine Grove Elementary was a Title I school receiving federal funding with a student population of about 1,400, whereas John. D. Floyd K-8 Environmental Science School was a non-Title I school with a student population up to 1,700 students. Principals and staff at both schools were committed to raising student achievement by improving instructional practices. Pine Grove received an "A" grade from the state for 6 consecutive years and made AYP for 2 consecutive years. John D. Floyd was awarded an "A" grade by the state for 4 consecutive years but did not make AYP. Following is a brief reflective discussion on possible reasons for the differences between these two good schools based on the correlate data.

Dave Dannemiller was the principal at Pine Grove for 9 years. When he arrived at Pine Grove, he found that many of its teachers had moved with his predecessor to a new school. Consequently, Dannemiller had to recruit new teachers. He used this to his advantage in revisiting the school mission. He worked purposefully and deliberately with teachers and parents to forge a school culture where student learning was the top priority. He set high expectations and created a culture over time in which teachers took ownership of student learning. He was noted for encouraging teachers, and he applauded effective teachers and set them as models and mentors for other teachers. His school exemplified an advanced level for many of the correlates.

Marcia Austin was the principal at John D. Floyd for 5 years. She inherited a growing school that had consistently made an "A" grade despite high teacher turnover, a rapidly changing student population, including a significant increase in students in exceptional education and students who were not fluent in English. Austin led the school through a pivotal transition from an elementary school to a K–8 school that included an environmental science program. Her main focus was on the school's purpose, with an emphasis on consistency of practice across grades and subjects. Her school exemplified some correlates at the advanced level and others at the proficient level.

Positive Home–School Relations

Dannemiller considered parental support to be critical to the school making AYP. He invited parents to functions and meetings and communicated school improvements to parents. He involved parents in decision making, letting them know that they had an active voice in the school. Dannemiller required parents to complete volunteer hours and rewarded them by allowing them to pick their child's teacher on a first-come, first-served basis. He emphasized strong teacher–parent relationships.

Austin introduced parent data review evenings, combining them with a social event at which food was served. She also introduced parent nights to discuss math and language arts data. Parents were visible as volunteers on campus. She required teachers to hold data team meetings prior to the years where standardized testing would be done. She communicated to parents through multiple means. She stressed an individualized approach to student learning. Austin's efforts paid off with increases in test scores. However, in the area of home–school relations, she admits that much more could have been done to boost parental involvement.

Opportunity to Learn and Student Time on Task

Both schools had clearly established routines and schedules and sought to guard instructional learning time by protecting the master schedule, monitoring all announcements, and limiting teacher meetings and classroom visits. Both schools built a cultural awareness of time pressure on the instructional day. Both schools had a 90-minute reading block and a 60-minute math block. To further safeguard teachers' instructional time, Dannemiller insisted that teacher meetings be scheduled at least 2 weeks in advance. Goodies for parties were only allowed at the end of the day.

Austin temporarily suspended electives for students requiring additional time in math, reading, and writing. She also provided additional opportunities for remediation after school. She admitted that a growing student population and the addition of the environmental center [in grades 5–8] resulted in many interruptions for student discipline. The burgeoning student population and increasing ESE student count posed a challenge when it came to meeting all the students' needs.

Climate of High Expectations

At Pine Grove, Dannemiller believed that the mission and vision statements set the tone for the entire school. He communicated high expectations for all students, including the students in exceptional education and students who were not native English speakers. He instituted a daily schoolwide recitation of the school's mission, which emphasized self-efficacy, or what the students could achieve. Teachers set up situations in which students felt empowered in their learning. Overall, an increasing percentage of teachers felt the school had a climate of high expectations.

At John D. Floyd, Austin also believed that the mission and vision statements were integral to the school's culture. However, there was a decreasing percentage of teachers who thought that the school had high expectations for all students. This may have been attributed to the significant increase in the student population, especially the population of students in ESE. It was felt that there were limited time and resources to meet the needs of the ESE population and comply with state mandates. Still, teachers were encouraged and empowered to set the bar high, especially during faculty meetings when the school's vision and mission were communicated.

Clear and Focused Mission

When Dannemiller became principal at Pine Grove, he revisited the school mission and worked collaboratively with the staff to create buy-in. He posted visible signs around the campus with the school mission. He constantly reminded staff that the mission had to be implemented daily. Conversations between the administration and staff centered on data, the school mission, and instructional strategies and trickled down to teacher and parent discussions about student improvement. He strongly encouraged teachers to keep things fresh and implement new ideas. The school mission even drove the school community and helped everyone to stay focused on student learning.

When Austin assumed the reins of principalship at John D. Floyd, she also revisited the mission and broadcast it. She had it posted throughout the school and placed on all school publications and letterheads. She focused on building a climate of equity and excellence, where all school personnel shared in the responsibility for educating students. She noted that there was room for improvement in sharing the mission with all the teachers.

Frequent Monitoring of Student Progress

Teachers monitored data using assessment software and explored ways to improve student scores in both case study schools. Both schools required teachers to be accountable for student learning and to use the data to drive instruction. The main differences appear to be subtle differences in the principals' approaches to this correlate. For example, Dannemiller personally held follow-up data meetings with teachers and asked them to show him how they were going to use the data to improve student learning. Gradually, teachers came to him of their own accord to show how data were being used to drive instruction.

At John D. Floyd, teachers were also expected to review data. They had a flow chart and checklist to help them gather pertinent student data. Data meetings were required across each grade level to discuss instructional strategies and recommendations for continuous improvement. Austin instituted multiple monitoring practices, including weekly monitoring of high-risk populations in primary grades, classroom assessments, benchmark assessments, and teachers' analysis and reflection of results. Both schools had data walls that displayed overall student growth and learning gains (without identifying students' names). Both schools were advanced in this correlate.

Instructional Leadership

Both case study principals described themselves as instructional leaders. Both held teachers accountable for student learning. Both principals ensured that everyone was working toward the same mission. Both principals practiced situational leadership, especially participatory leadership. However, they were willing to provide direct leadership where warranted.

Dannemiller emphasized servant leadership and went out of his way to meet teachers' needs by providing resources and practical assistance to help teachers improve student learning. He focused on motivating teachers by supporting them and leading them in discussions about student achievement and the use of appropriate instructional strategies.

Austin also displayed servant leadership. She modeled her expectations for teachers and team leaders. Her principal focus was on the students and instructional practices to increase student achievement. The goal at both schools was to build cultures of shared learning and collaboration. Correlate survey results from both schools revealed a drop in the percentage of teachers who believed this correlate was strongly evident. Perhaps a partial explanation for this correlate drop may have been because of increased demands on teachers by the principals and staff turnover (especially at John D. Floyd).

Safe and Orderly Environment

Both case study schools had large numbers of students. They had clearly communicated and enforced policies for making the transition between classes and to key destination points. Dannemiller emphasized a school-wide positive reinforcement reward system in which students were rewarded by any school personnel for doing what was expected. Teachers were held accountable for following classroom procedures and attempting to change the behavior of students before sending them to the office. At John D. Floyd, students were taught how to make the transition from point A to point B from kindergarten. School rules were posted. Teachers were expected to develop positive relationships with students and to be in control of the classroom. After the addition of the environmental center and a resource officer, the staff's perception of the safe and orderly environment correlate dropped significantly.

Summary

The school correlates are purposefully enforced in proficient-level schools like John D. Floyd. Full operationalization of the correlates results in advanced-level schools such as Pine Grove. Stable principal leadership; collaboration with teachers, parents, and the community; time; and the deliberate operationalization of correlate strategies are key ingredients that can help any school become a proficient- and then an advanced-level school. However, much needs to be taken into consideration when comparing schools: 1) consistency of the instructional leadership, 2) student population, 3) resources, and 4) instructional practices. Both Pine Grove and John D. Floyd demonstrate the ongoing need for instructional leaders to examine the correlates and use them as a barometer to improve in key areas that will affect student achievement. Both schools also demonstrate the collaboration and relationship that must occur among all stakeholders to ensure that a school not only makes an "A" grade but also continues to move forward in this era of transparency and accountability.

REVISITING THE CORRELATE STRATEGIES

Edmonds (1979b) was a forerunner in identifying factors co-related to student learning. These "co-related" variables became known as the "co-relates" or "correlates" of effective schools and were refined over time. They include 1) Positive Home–School Relations, 2) Opportunity to Learn and Student Time on Task, 3) Climate of High Expectations, 4) Clear and Focused Mission, 5) Frequent Monitoring of Student Progress, 6) Instructional Leadership, and 7) Safe and Orderly Environment. Chapters 3–9 of this book focused on these correlates by presenting vignettes, strategies for applying the correlates to improve student achievement, frontline perspectives, supportive research, and case studies.

Key Lessons

There are many lessons to be learned from the research and experience of educators on the front lines. Examples follow:

1. Each of the seven correlates is a characteristic of an effective school.
2. Effective schools have a strong presence of the correlates.
3. There are two levels of the correlates: proficient or first-generation correlates are the "letter of the law" enforced correlates, whereas advanced or second-generation correlates are the "spirit of the law" correlates that are part of the culture of the school.
4. Educators can boost the presence of the correlates by operationalizing the correlates.
5. Applying the correlate strategies at each of the three levels (district, school, and classroom) is operationalizing the correlates.

6. The correlates are interdependent. Therefore, boosting the presence of a few targeted correlates can have the effect of boosting others, too.

7. The Positive Home School–Relations correlate is the number one predictor of student academic achievement, including AYP scores.

THE AYP GAME . . . APPEAL

The NCLB call is clear and has penetrated the ionosphere of education. School leaders must ensure that all students and subgroups of students demonstrate adequate annual learning gains or face consequences. Educators can no longer sit back and pretend that the era of accountability is just another fad and will eventually fade away. They can no longer afford to say that this child is not my responsibility or that child should be sent to another school so that my school can achieve a certain standardized test score. They can no longer invest time in playing number games with subgroups or teaching to the test, when the stakes are so high. They cannot afford to be complacent if one school in their district does not make AYP, because those students are *their* students and it is not just that principal's or just that school's problem.

Exhortation

We as educators must exhaust every effort in trying to help students, teachers, and principals to be successful, even if they are not in our district; we must embrace our advantage of being a collective force of educators who should utilize every research-based practice, every time-tested instructional strategy, and every basic common-sense method to ensure that no child feels as if he or she is a failure or does not have the potential to learn. The challenge is great, but we as educators have the resources and collective capability to meet it. Each of us has been uniquely gifted and equipped to meet the AYP and student achievement crisis of the hour. The future of our students and the future of America rides on the shoulders of educators today. Edmonds reminds us that we already possess what we need to make a difference in the lives of students:

> We can, whenever and wherever we choose, successfully teach all children whose schooling is of interest to us. We already know more than we need to do that. Whether or not we do it must finally depend on how we feel about the fact that we haven't so far. (1979b, p. 35)

The Challenge

America's schools stand at the dusk of the NCLB era with the dawn of the reauthorization of ESEA just around the corner. The achievement crisis continues. Schools are still responsible for the bottom line—student learning—as measured by state assessment scores.

The education machinery is complex. Change takes time, money, legislation, and leadership. Most of all, it takes the combined effort of dedicated educators who continue to go above and beyond to ensure that each student learns and that every student makes AYP.

The clarion call of the hour and our challenge to readers is to focus on what really works: the correlates. They are supported by the test of time and nearly 4 decades of research. They are the blueprint for what makes great schools great. Most important, they have been linked to AYP scores.

Educators are the key to maximizing students' learning, by ensuring that no child is left behind and by providing a world-class education for students. Highly effective educators are cognizant of the complex interplay of the seven correlates of effective schools, use data-driven methods to accurately assess their school's or district's priority needs, identify all key correlates that will bring the highest achievement return on time invested, and use precision remediation to ensure learning for all. When we steer our educational ship according to the solidly grounded and researched fundamentals, we steer by correlate beacons of hope and ensure that our schools are schools that make the grade.

CHAPTER REFLECTION

1. Discuss your response to the chapter prompt, "Nothing creative happens until energy is forced into a discipline" (Cook, 2000, p. 115). How does this quote apply to the operationalization of the correlates? Will they ever be operationalized if the correlate strategies are not deliberately put into practice? Explain.

2. Write a brief review of the AYP and student achievement crisis. What is it? What part does NCLB play in addressing this crisis? Give two or three examples.

3. The authors assert that "the way to work smarter and to see sustained increases in student learning and student achievement scores . . . is to purposefully cultivate a strong presence of the correlates in schools." Is this assertion research based? Explain. How would you cultivate a strong presence of the correlates in your position of influence? Give two or three research-backed correlate strategies. Say why you selected them and how you would implement them.

4. What lessons have you learned from the case study reflections? What correlate strategies did Pine Grove use that John D. Floyd did not? How would you rate these schools in their effectiveness? Why?

5. What will you do in your capacity as an educator to ensure that your current or future school will make the grade? Outline a strategy that you will use. Give your rationale for this strategy.

6. Write an encouraging (and attractive) note to a peer or supervisor sincerely thanking him or her for all the energies and talents he or she uses in making a difference in the lives of students. Make several specific notes of praiseworthy endeavors you have noticed. Give the note to this person.

7. How will you personally answer the challenge outlined in the concluding section of this chapter? Support your response with grounded rationale and examples.

References

Akiba, M., LeTendre, G.K., & Scribner, J.P. (2007). Teacher quality, opportunity gap, and national achievement in 46 countries. *Educational Researcher, 36*(7), 369–387.

American Bar Association. (2001). *Zero tolerance policy.* Retrieved September 24, 2010, from http://www.abanet.org/crimjust/juvjus/zerotolreport.html

American Psychological Association. (2006). *Are zero tolerance policies effective in the schools?* Retrieved September 24, 2010, from http://www.apa.org/pubs/info/reports/zero-tolerance.pdf

American Recovery and Reinvestment Act of 2009, PL 111-5.

Anderson, D. (2006). In or out: Surprises in reading comprehension instruction. *Intervention in School and Clinic, 41*(3), 175–179. Retrieved March 4, 2007, from Academic Search Premier database.

Anderson, G.L. (2002). A critique of the test for school leaders. *Educational Leadership, 59*(8), 67–70.

Ansalone, G. (2004). Educational opportunity and access to knowledge: Tracking in the U.S. and Japan. *Race, Gender, and Class, 11*(3), 140–152.

Association for Effective Schools, Inc. (n.d.). *Effective school surveys.* Retrieved January 12, 2011, from http://www.mes.org/surveys.html

Bamburg, J.D., & Andrews, R.L. (1991). *Instructional leadership, school goals, and student achievement: Exploring the relationship between means and ends. An overview* (ERIC Document Reproduction Service No. ED319783).

Ban, J.R. (2000). *Parents assuring student success.* Bloomington, IN: T.G. Design Group.

Bandura, A. (1997). *Self-efficacy: The exercise of control.* New York: W.H. Freeman.

Bandura, A. (2001). Social cognitive theory: An agentic perspective. *Annual Review of Psychology, 52*(1), 1.

Bandura, A., & Locke, E.A. (2003). Negative self-efficacy and goal effects revisited. *Journal of Applied Psychology, 88*(1), 87–89.

Barth, R. (1990). *Improving schools from within: Teachers, parents, and principals can make a difference.* San Francisco: Jossey-Bass.

Bedford, B. (1988). *School effectiveness and student achievement: A study of relationships in Georgia middle schools* (ERIC Document Reproduction Service No. ED303898).

Beers, K. (2003). *When kids can't read: What teachers can do.* Portsmouth, NH: Heinemann.

Bennis, W., & Goldsmith, J. (2003). *Learning to lead.* New York: Perseus Books.

Blackburn, B. (2005). *Classroom motivation from A to Z: How to engage your students in learning.* New York: Eye on Education.

Blanchard, K., & Hodges, P. (2005). *Lead like Jesus.* Nashville: Thomas Nelson.

Blankstein, A.M. (2004). *Failure is not an option.* Thousand Oaks, CA: Corwin Press.

Bloom, S.B. (1968). Learning for mastery. *Evaluation Comment, 1*(2). Retrieved January 13, 2011, from http://www.cse.ucla.edu/products/evaluation/cresst_ec1968_m.pdf

Boaler, J. (2006). How a detracked mathematics approach promoted respect, responsibility, and high achievement. *Theory into Practice, 45*(1), 40–46. Retrieved March 4, 2007, from Academic Search Premier database.

Bohanon, H., Flannery, K., Malloy, J., & Fenning, P. (2009). Utilizing positive behavior supports in high school settings to improve school completion rates for students with high incidence conditions. *Exceptionality, 17*(1), 30–44.

Boston College, Lynch School of Education. (1999). *Trends in Mathematics and Science Achievement (TIMSS, 1999).* Retrieved January 3, 2011, from http://timss.bc.edu/timss1999.html

Brace, N., Kemp, R., & Snelgar, N. (2006). *SPSS for psychologists: A guide to data analysis using SPSS for Windows, version 12 and 13* (3rd ed.). New York: Palgrave Macmillan.

Brandt, S. (2003). What parents really want out of parent-teacher conferences. *Kappa Delta Pi Record, 39*(4), 1–4.

Brewster, C., & Railsback, J. (2005, November). *Leadership practices of successful principals.* Portland, OR: Northwest Regional Educational Laboratory.

Brookover, W.B., Beady, C., Flood, P., Schweitzer, J., & Wisebaker, J. (1979). *Schools, social systems and student achievement: Schools can make a difference.* New York: Praeger.

Brookover, W.B., & Lezotte, L. (1979). *Changes in characteristics coincident with changes in school achievement* (Occasional Paper No. 17. ED 181005). East Lansing, MI: Michigan State University, Institute for Research on Teaching.

Brown v. Board of Education, 347 U.S. 483 (1954).

Brown, H., & Ciuffetelli Parker, D.C. (Eds.). (2009). *Foundational methods: Understanding teaching and learning.* Toronto: Pearson Education.

Bulach, C., & Potter, L. (2001). Dos and don'ts of parent-teacher conferences. *The Education Digest, 66*(9), 37–40.

Burris, C., & Welner, K. (2005). Closing the achievement gap by detracking. *Phi Delta Kappan, 86*(8), 594–598. Retrieved March 4, 2007, from Academic Search Premier database.

Caldwell, J., Huitt, W., & Graeber, A. (1982). Time spent in learning: Implications from research. *Elementary School Journal, 82*(5), 471–480.

California Center for Effective Schools. (2009). *Connections for success.* Retrieved August 5, 2010, from http://effectiveschools.education.ucsb.edu/correlates.html

Cardella, F., & Sudlow, R.E. (2000). *More Effective Schools Survey.* Stuyvesant, NY: Association for Effective Schools.

Cawelti, G., & Protheroe, N. (2001). *High student achievement: How six school districts changed into high-performance systems.* Arlington, VA: Educational Research Service.

Center for Comprehensive School Reform and Improvement. (2009). *Developing a positive school climate.* Retrieved July 24, 2010, from www.centerforcsri.org

Central Advisory Council for Education. (1967). *Children and their primary schools (Plowden report).* Redwood City, CA: Pendragon House.

Chall, J.S. (2000). *The academic achievement challenge: What really works in the classroom.* New York: The Guilford Press.

Chard, D. (2004). Toward a science of professional development in early reading instruction. *Exceptionality, 12*(3), 175–191.

Chen, G. (2009). Is your public school's zero-tolerance policy punishing innocent students? *Public School Review*. Retrieved January 5, 2011, from http://www.public schoolreview.com/articles/111

Christie, K. (2005). Changing the nature of parent involvement. *Phi Delta Kappan, 86*(9), 645–646.

Civil Rights Act of 1964, PL 88-352, 20 U.S.C. §§ 241 *et seq.*

Clark, D., & Linn, M.C. (2003). Designing for knowledge integration: The impact of instructional time. *The Journal of the Learning Sciences, 12*(4), 451–493.

Clarke, S., & Dunlap, G. (2008). A descriptive analysis of intervention research published in the Journal of Positive Behavior Interventions: 1999 through 2005. *Journal of Positive Behavior Interventions, 10*(1), 67–71. Retrieved June 3, 2009, from Academic Search Complete database.

Coelho, E. (1998). *Teaching and learning in multicultural schools: An integrated approach.* Clevedon, United Kingdom: Philadelphia Multilingual Matters.

Cohn, A.M. (2001). *Positive behavior support: Information for educators.* Retrieved September 24, 2010, from http://www.nasponline.org/resources/factsheets/pbs_fs.aspx

Cole, S.A. (2003). *Correlates of effective schools as predictors of elementary magnet school academic success.* Unpublished doctoral dissertation, University of Louisiana at Monroe.

Coleman, J.S., Campbell, E.Q., Hobson, C.J., McPartland, J., Mood, A.M., Weinfield, F.D., et al. (1966). *Equality of educational opportunity.* Washington, DC: U.S. Government Printing Office.

Cook, W.J., Jr. (2000). *Strategics: The art and science of holistic strategy.* Westport, CT: Quorum Books.

Cooper, H., Charlton, K., Valentine, J., & Muhlenbruck, L. (2000). *Making the most of summer school: A meta-analytic and narrative review* (Monograph Series for The Society for Research in Child Development, Vol. 65[1], Serial no. 260). Ann Arbor, MI: Society for Research in Child Development.

Cordry, S., & Wilson, J. (2004). Parents as first teachers. *Education, 125*(1), 56–62.

Cotton, K. (2003). *Principals and student achievement: What the research says.* Alexandria, VA: Association for Supervision and Curriculum Development (ASCD).

Council of Chief State School Officers. (2008). *Interstate School Leaders Licensure Consortium (ISLLC) standards for school leaders.* Washington, DC: Author.

Covey, S. (1989). *The seven habits of highly effective people.* New York: Simon and Schuster.

Creemers, P.M.B. (2002). From school effectiveness and school improvement to effective school improvement: Background, theoretical analysis, and outline of the empirical study. *Educational Research and Evaluation: An International Journal on Theory and Practice, 8,* 343–362.

Crew, R. (2007). *Only connect: The way to save our schools.* New York: Sarah Crichton Books.

Cummins, J. (2006). *BICS and CALP explained.* Retrieved December 3, 2006, from http://www.iteachilearn.com/cummins/bicscalp.html

Curriculum Review. (2005). Schools get creative to connect with parents. *Curriculum Review, 44*(8), 11.

Daly, A.J., & Chrispeels, J.H. (2006, January). *Educational accountability: Leading in a context of threat.* Paper presented to the 19th International Congress for School Effectiveness and Improvement, Fort Lauderdale, FL.

Darling-Hammond, L. (2000). *Solving the dilemmas of teacher supply, demand, and standards: How we can ensure a competent, caring, and qualified teacher for every child.* New York: National Commission on Teaching's Future.

Darling-Hammond, L., & Youngs, P. (2002). Defining highly qualified teachers: What does scientifically-based research actually tell us? (ERIC Document Reproduction Service No. EJ662187). *Educational Researcher, 31*(9), 13–25. Retrieved October 21, 2007, from ERIC database.

deFur, S., & Korinek, L. (2006). *Getting the right data.* Williamsburg, VA: The Training and Technical Assistance Center, William and Mary School of Education T/TAC Link Lines. Retrieved January 14, 2011, from http://education.wm.edu/centers/ttac/resources/articles/assessment/getrightdata/index.php

DeMoss, K. (2005). How arts integration supports student learning: Evidence from students in Chicago's CAPE partnership schools. *Arts and Learning Research Journal, 21*(1), 91–118. Retrieved June 2, 2009, from Education Research Complete database.

Diaz-Rico, L., & Weed, K. (2005). *The crosscultural, language, and academic development handbook: A complete K-12 reference guide* (2nd ed.). Boston: Allyn & Bacon.

Dieker, L.A., & Ousley, D. M. (2006). Speaking the same language: Bringing together highly qualified secondary English and special education teachers. *TEACHING Exceptional Children Plus, 2*(4) Article 3. Retrieved January 17, 2011, from http://escholarship.bc.edu/education/tecplus/vol2/iss4/art3

Discovery Education. (2007). *About ThinkLink.* Retrieved from http://www.thinklinklearning.com/about.php

Donderlinger, D.J. (1986). *Learning made simple: Tools to improve your learning skills.* Sioux Falls, SC: Donderlinger.

Duran, A. (2005, January). Factors to consider when evaluating school accountability results. *Journal of Law and Education.* Retrieved January 20, 2011, from http://findarticles.com/p/articles/mi_qa3994/is_200501/ai_n9483806

Dwyer, K., & Osher, D. (2000). *Safeguarding our children: An action guide.* Retrieved September 24, 2010, from http://www2.ed.gov/admins/lead/safety/actguide/action_guide.pdf

Eaker, R., DuFour, R., & DuFour, R. (2002). *Getting started: Reculturing schools to become professional learning communities.* Bloomington, IN: Solution Tree Press.

Edmonds, R.R. (1979a). *A discussion of the literature and issues related to effective schooling.* Cambridge, MA: Harvard Graduate School of Education, Center for Urban Studies.

Edmonds, R.R. (1979b). Effective schools for the urban poor. *Educational Leadership, 37*(10), 15–24.

Edmonds, R.R., & Frederiksen, J.R. (1978). *Search for effective schools: The identification and analysis of city schools that are instructionally effective for poor children.* Cambridge, MA: Harvard University, Center for Urban Studies.

Education Policy Institute. (2005). *Focus on results: An academic impact analysis of the knowledge is power program (KIPP).* Virginia Beach, VA: Author.

Educational Testing Service. (2003). *Parsing the achievement gap II.* Retrieved January 4, 2011, from http://www.ets.org/Media/Education_Topics/pdf/parsing.pdf

Effective Schools (n.d.). *Effective Schools.* Retrieved on January 13, 2011, from http://www.effectiveschools.com/

Eisenberger, J., Cont-D'Antiono, M., & Bertrando, R. (2000). *Self-efficacy: Raising the bar for students with learning needs.* Larchmont, NY: Eye on Education.

Elbaum, B., Vaughn, S., Hughes, M., Moody, S., & Schumm, J. (2000). How reading outcomes of students with disabilities are related to instructional grouping formats: A meta analytic review. In R. Gersten, E. Schiller, & S. Vaughn (Eds.), *Contemporary special education research: Synthesis of the knowledge base on critical educational issues* (pp.105–136). Mahwah, NJ: Lawrence Erlbaum Associates.

Elbow, P. (2004). Writing first. *Educational Leadership, 62*(2), 9–13.

Elementary and Secondary Education Act of 1965, PL 89-10, 20 U.S.C. §§ 241 *et seq.*

Elliot, I. (1996, February). Dads by the dozen. *Teaching PreK-8, 26*, 54–55.

Emmer, T.E., & Hickman, J. (1991). Teacher efficacy in classroom management and discipline. *Educational and Psychological Measurement, 51*(3), 755–765.

Endress, S., Weston, H., Marchand-Martella, N., Martella, R., & Simmons, J. (2007). Examining the effects of Phono-Graphix on the remediation of reading skills of students with disabilities: A program evaluation. *Education and Treatment of Children, 30*(2), 1–20. Retrieved June 2, 2009, from SocINDEX with Full Text database.

Engelmann, S. (2007). *Teaching needy kids in our backward system.* Eugene, OR: ADI Press.

Family Involvement Partnership for Learning. (1998). *Steps you can take to improve your children's education.* Retrieved January 5, 2011, from http://www2.ed.gov/pubs/PFIE/families.html

Farbman, D., & Kaplan, C. (2005). *Time for a change: The promise of extended time.* Boston, MA: Schools for Promoting Student Achievement.

Feuerstein, A. (2000). School characteristics and parental involvement: Influences on participation in children's schools. *The Journal of Educational Research, 94*(1), 29–39.

Fisher, D., Frey, N., & Williams, D. (2003). It takes us all. *Principal Leadership, 4*(3), 41–44.

Flaherty, S., & Hackler, R. (2010, May 1). *Exploring the effects of differentiated instruction and cooperative learning on the intrinsic motivational behaviors of elementary reading students.* Retrieved from http://www.eric.ed.gov:80/ERICWebPortal/search/detailmini.jsp?_nfpb=true&_&ERICExtSearch_SearchValue_0=ED509195&ERICExtSearch_SearchType_0=no&accno=ED509195

Flanagain, W.C. (2007). *A survey—The negative aspects of in and out of school suspensions and alternatives that promote academic achievement.* Retrieved from http://www.eric.ed.gov/PDFS/ED499538.pdf

Florida Department of Education. (2010). *School accountability reports.* Retrieved from http://schoolgrades.fldoe.org/default.asp

Florida Department of Education, Bureau of K-12 Assessment. (2010). *Florida Comprehensive Assessment Test (FCAT).* Retrieved January 3, 2011, from http://fcat.fldoe.org/fcat

Fulgham, R. (2004). *All I really need to know I learned in kindergarten* (Rev. ed.). New York: Ballantine Books.

Fullan, M. (1997). *What's worth fighting for in your school?* New York: Teachers College Press.

Fullan, M. (2001). *Leading in a culture of change.* San Francisco: Jossey-Bass.

Gehrke, R. (2005). Poor schools, poor students, successful teachers. *Kappa Delta Pi Record, 42*(1), 14. Retrieved March 04, 2007, from the ERIC database.

Georgia Department of Education. (n.d.). *Criterion-Referenced Competency Test.* Retrieved January 3, 2011, from http://www.gadoe.org/ci_testing.aspx?PageReq=CI_TESTING_CRCT

Gerstner, L. (2002). *Who says elephants can't fly? Inside IBM's historic turnaround.* New York: Harper Business.

Ginott, H.G., Ginott, A., & Goddard, H.W. (Eds.). (2003). *Between parent and child: The best-selling classic that revolutionized parent-child communication* (Rev. ed.). New York: Three Rivers Press.

Glasser, W. (1998). *Choice theory in the classroom.* New York: HarperPerennial.

Goldhaber, D. (2003). *Indicators of teacher quality* (Report No. ED478408-2003-07-00). New York: ERIC Clearinghouse of Urban Education.

Graham, S., & Harris, K. (1989). Improving learning disabled students' skills at composing essays: Self-instructional strategy training. *Exceptional Children, 56*(3), 201–214. Retrieved September 24, 2008, from Academic Search Premier database.

Gray, D. (2009). A new look at instructional leadership (ISLLC Standard 1 Principal Preparation Programs; Case Study). *Alabama International Journal of Educational Leadership Preparation, 4*(1), 1–4.

Greenleaf, R.K. (2002). *Servant leadership: A journey into the nature and legitimate power of greatness.* Mahwah, NJ: Paulist Press.

Grissom, J.A. & Loeb, S. (2009). *Triangulating principal effectiveness: How perspectives of parents, teachers, and assistant principals identify the central importance of managerial skills* (School Leadership Research Report No. 09-1). Stanford, CA: Stanford University, Institute for Research on Education Policy & Practice.

Hallinger, P., Bickman, L., & Davis, K. (1996). School context, principal leadership, and student reading achievement. *Elementary School Journal, 96*, 527–549.

Hannaford, C. (2005). *Smart moves: Why learning is not all in your head* (2nd ed.). Salt Lake City, UT: Great River Books.

Hawes, C., & Plourde, L. (2005). Parental involvement and its influence on the reading achievement of 6th grade students. *Reading Involvement, 42*(1), 47–57.

Hill, N. (1928). *The law of success in sixteen lessons: Teaching for the first time in the history of the world, the true philosophy upon which all personal success is built.* Meriden, CT: Ralston University Press.

Hirsh, S. (1996, September). Seeing and creating the future. *School Team Innovator.* National Staff Development Council.

Hofferth, S.L., & Sandberg, J. (2001). How American children spend their time. *Journal of Marriage and Family, 63*, 295–308.

Houtenville, A.J., & Conway, K.S. (2008). Parental effort, school resources, and student achievement. *Journal of Human Resources, 43*(2), 437–453.

Huitt, W. (2006). Overview of classroom processes. *Educational Psychology Interactive.* Valdosta, GA: Valdosta State University. Retrieved from http://chiron .valdosta.edu/whuitt/col/process/class.html

Illinois State Board of Education. (n.d.). *No child left behind/adequate yearly progress.* Retrieved September 25, 2010, from http://www.isbe.state.il.us/ayp/htmls/ glossary.htm

Iowa Department of Education. (n.d.). *Students Assessment. Iowa Test of Basic Skills.* Retrieved from http://www.iowa.gov/educate/index.php?option=com_content &view=article&id=1043&Itemid=1485

Jacobson, A.L., Huffman, J.B., & Rositas de Cantu, M.C. (1998). Parent involvement training with Hispanic parents. *The Delta Kappa Gamma Bulletin, 65*(1), 30–37.

Jencks, C., Smith, M.S., Acland, H., Bane, M.J., Cohen, D., Grintlis, H., et al. (1972). *Inequality: A reassessment of the effects of family and schooling in America.* New York: Basic Books.

Jensen, A.R. (1969). How much can we boost I.Q. and scholastic achievement? *Harvard Educational Review, 39*(1), 1–123.

Johnson, J.A., Musial, D.L., Hall, G.E., & Gollnick, D.M. (2011). *Foundations of American education: Perspectives on education in a changing world* (15th ed.). New York: Pearson.

Jones, L. (1996). *The path: Creating your mission statement for work and for life.* New York: Hyperion.

Jones, V., & Jones L. (2010). Creating positive peer relationships. In L. Jones & V. Jones (Eds.), *Comprehensive classroom management: Creating communities of support and solving problems* (9th ed., pp. 99–134). Upper Saddle River, NJ: Merrill.

Jordan, A., Kirkcaly-Iftar, G., & Diamond, C.T.P. (1993). Who has the problem, the student or the teacher? Differences in teacher beliefs about their work with at-risk and integrated exceptional students. *International Journal of Disability, Development and Education, 40*, 45–62.

Kagan, S. (2002, Summer). Kagan structures for English language learners. *Kagan Online Magazine*. Retrieved January 19, 2011, from http://www.kaganonline.com/free_articles/dr_spencer_kagan/ASK17.php

Kagan, S., & Kagan, M. (2008). *Kagan cooperative learning—Resources for teachers*. San Clemente, CA: Kagan Publishing.

Kates, A., & Klassen, R. (2007). *Motivation, job stress, and job satisfaction of special education teachers*. Retrieved June 3, 2009, from http://www.apa.org/pubs/databases/psycextra/index.aspx

Keedy, J.L., & McDonald, D.H. (2006, January). *Tough times or the best of times?* Paper presented to the 19th International Congress for School Effectiveness and Improvement, Fort Lauderdale, FL. Retrieved from http://icee.isu.edu/JES Issues/JES%202004v3.1/1tough20043.1.pdf

Keenan, D. (n.d.). *Mission-driven organization*. Retrieved May 6, 2011, from http://www.acsi.org/LinkClick.aspx?fileticket=eKme4jlARWg%3D&tabid=681

Kirschenbaum, H. (1999). Night and day: Succeeding with parents at school. *Principal, 78*(3), 20–23.

Kozol, J. (2005). *The shame of the nation: The restoration of apartheid schooling in America*. New York: Crown Publishers.

Kyriakides, L., & Luyten, H. (2006, January). *Using different methodological approaches and criteria to measure the effect of schooling: Implications for the development of educational and effectiveness research*. Paper presented at the 19th International Congress for School Effectiveness and Improvement, Fort Lauderdale, FL.

Larkin, M. (2002). *Using scaffolded instruction to optimize learning* (ERIC Document Reproduction Service No. ED474301).

Lashway, L. (1997). *Leading with vision*. Eugene, OR: ERIC Clearinghouse on Educational Management.

Lazar, A., Broderick, P., Mastrilli, T., & Slostad, F. (1999). Educating teachers for parent involvement. *Contemporary Education, 70*(3), 5–10.

Leaf, C. (2008). *Who switched off my brain: Controlling toxic thoughts and emotions*. Nashville, TN: Thomas Nelson.

Leithwood, K.A., & Riehl, C. (2003). *What we know about successful school leadership*. Philadelphia: Laboratory for Students Success, Temple University.

Levine, U.D., & Lezotte, L.W. (1990). *Unusually effective schools: A review and analysis of research and practice*. Madison, WI: National Center for Effective Schools Research and Development.

Lewis, S.G., & Batts, K. (2005). How to implement differentiated instruction? Adjust, adjust, adjust. *Journal of Staff Development, 26*(4), 26–31.

Lezotte, L.W. (1991). *Correlates of effective schools: The first and second generation*. Retrieved January 17, 2011, from http://www.effectiveschools.com/images/stories/escorrelates.pdf

Lezotte, L.W. (1997). *Learning for all*. Okemos, MI: Effective School Products.

Lezotte, L.W. (2002). *Needs assessment systems: Issues of reliability and validity*. Okemos, MI: Effective Schools Products.

Lezotte, L., Edmonds, R., & Ratner, G. (1974). *Remedy for school failure to equitably deliver basic school skills*. Cambridge, MA: Harvard University, Center for Urban Studies.

Lezotte, L.W. & McKee, K.M. (2002). *Assembly required: A continuous school improvement system*. Okemos, MI: Effective Schools Products.

Linek, W.M., Rasinski, T.V., & Harkins, D.M. (1997) Teacher perceptions of parent involvement in literacy education. *Reading Horizons, 38*, 90–107.

Lotan, R. (2006). Teaching teachers to build equitable classrooms. *Theory Into Practice, 45*(1), 32–39. Retrieved March 4, 2007, from the Academic Search Premier database.

Louisiana Department of Education. (n.d.). *Accountability. Louisiana Educational Assessment Program.* Retrieved from http://www.louisianaschools.net/lde/portals/accountability.html

Luiselli, J., Putnam, R., Handler, M., & Feinberg, A. (2005). Whole-school positive behaviour support: Effects on student discipline problems and academic performance. *Educational Psychology, 25*(2/3), 183–198.

Lyle, S. (1999). An investigation of pupil perceptions of mixed-ability grouping to enhance literacy in children aged 9–10. *Educational Studies, 25*(3), 283–296. Retrieved March 4, 2007, from the Academic Search Premier database.

Malone, Y. (2002). Social cognitive theory and the choice theory: A compatibility analysis. *International Journal of Reality Therapy, 22*(1), 10–13.

Manning, M.L., & Bucher, K.T. (2003). *Classroom management: Models, applications and cases.* Upper Saddle River, NJ: Prentice Hall.

Margolis, H., & McCabe, P. (2006). Improving self-efficacy and motivation: What to do, what to say. *Intervention in School and Clinic, 41*(4), 218–227. Retrieved June 3, 2009, from Academic Search Complete database.

MarketingTeacher.com (n.d.). *History of the SWOT analysis.* Retrieved March 11, 2011, from http://www.marketingteacher.com/swot/history-of-swot.html

Marks, H.M., & Printy, S.M. (2003). Principal leadership and school performance: An integration of transformational and instructional leadership. *Education Administration Quarterly, 30,* 370–379.

Marzano, R.J. (2003). *What works in schools: Translating research into action.* Alexandria, VA: ASCD.

Marzano, R. (2007). *The art and science of teaching.* Alexandria, VA: ASCD.

Marzano, R.J., Waters, T., & McNulty, B.A., (2005). *School leadership that works: From research to results.* Alexandria, VA: ASCD.

Mason, C., Steedly, K., & Thormann, M. (2008). Impact of arts integration on voice, choice, and access. *Teacher Education and Special Education, 31*(1), 36–46. Retrieved June 2, 2009, from Education Research Complete database.

Maxwell, J.C. (1998). *The 21 irrefutable laws of leadership.* Nashville: Thomas Nelson.

McGill, A. (1999). *Molly Bannaky.* New York: Houghton Mifflin Company.

Meichenbaum, D. (n.d.). *How educators can nurture resilience in high-risk families and their children.* Retrieved September 24, 2010, from http://www.teachsafeschools.org/Resilience.pdf

Mid-continent Research for Education and Learning. (2003). *Policy brief: School, teacher, and leadership impacts on student achievement.* Retrieved July 22, 2010, from http://www.mcrel.org/pdf/policybriefs/5032pi_pbschoolteacherleaderbrief.pdf

Missouri Department of Elementary and Secondary Education. (2010). *Mission.* Retrieved January 17, 2011, from http://dese.mo.gov/mission.html

Montana Safe Schools Center. (n.d.). *Safe schools assessment and resource bank (SSARB).* Retrieved September 24, 2010, from http://www.iersum.org/Montana_Safe_Schools_Center/Safe_Schools_Assessment_SSARB

Mortimore, P., Sammons, P., Stoll, L., Lewis, D., & Ecob, R. (1988). *School matters.* Berkeley, CA: The University of California Press.

National Association of School Psychologists. (2001). *Zero tolerance and alternative strategies: A fact sheet for educators and policymakers.* Retrieved September 24, 2010, from http://www.nasponline.org/resources/factsheets/zt_fs.aspx

National Center for Education Statistics. (n.d.). *Program for International Student Achievement (PISA).* Retrieved January 3, 2011, from http://nces.ed.gov/surveys/pisa

National Center for Education Statistics. (1997). *National study links father's involvement to children getting A's in school.* Retrieved May 27, 2005, from http://nces.ed.gov/pressrelease/father.asp

National Center on Student Progress Monitoring. (2009, para. 4). *Common questions for progress monitoring: What are the benefits of progress monitoring?* Retrieved January 17, 2011, from http://www.studentprogress.org/progresmon.asp#2

National Defense Education Act of 1958, PL 85-864. United States Statutes at Large, Vol. 72, p. 1580–1605.

National Education Commission on Time and Learning. (1994). *Prisoners of time: Report of the National Education Commission on Time and Learning.* Washington, DC: Author.

National Law Enforcement and Corrections Technology Center. (2003, Winter). Safe schools: A technology primer. *Tech Beat.* Retrieved September 24, 2010, from http://www.justnet.org/TechBeat%20Files/SafeSchWint03.pdf

National Public Radio. (2010, April 19). *Duncan prescribes drastic measures for schools.* Retrieved from http://www.npr.org/templates/story/story.php?storyId=126111829

Nesselrodt, P.S. (2006, January). *Ramping up to meet mandates of the No Child Left Behind Act by creating an ESL program reflecting effective schools research.* Paper presented at the19th International Congress for School Effectiveness and Improvement, Fort Lauderdale, FL. Retrieved from http://www.eric.ed.gov/ERICWeb Portal/search/detailmini.jsp?_nfpb=true&_&ERICExtSearch_SearchValue_0= EJ784210&ERICExtSearch_SearchType_0=no&accno=EJ784210

New York City Board of Education, Brooklyn Division of Assessment and Accountability. (2000). *Impact of teacher certification on reading and mathematics performance in elementary and middle schools in New York City schools.* New York: Author.

NGA Center for Best Practices. (2009). *Issue brief: Reducing dropout rates through expanded learning opportunities.* Retrieved September 25, 2010, from http://www .eric.ed.gov/PDFS/ED507637.pdf

Nicholas, K. (2002). *The effects of structured writing strategy training on expository compositions produced by African-American college students with learning disabilities* (Doctoral dissertation, Florida State University, 2002). Retrieved September 24, 2008, from Dissertations & Theses: Full Text database (Publication No. AAT 3072009).

Nichols-Solomon, R. (2001, January). Barriers to serious parent involvement. *The Education Digest, 66,* 33–37.

No Child Left Behind Act of 2001, PL 107-110, 115 Stat. 1425, 20 U.S.C. §§ 6301 *et seq.*

Noguera, P. (2003). *City schools and the American dream: Reclaiming the promise of public education.* New York: Teachers College Press.

Norton, M.I. (2003). Let's keep our quality school principals on the job. *High School Journal, 86*(2), 50–57.

Office of Educational Assessment. (n.d.). *Understanding item analysis reports.* Retrieved January 15, 2011, from http://www.washington.edu/oea/services/scanning_scoring/ scoring/item_analysis.html

Ormrod, J.E. (2009). *Human learning.* Upper Saddle River, NJ: Pearson Education.

Osher, D., Dwyer, K., & Jimerson, S. (2006). Safe, supportive and effective schools: Promoting school success to reduce school violence. In S. Jimerson & M. Furlong (Eds.), *Handbook of School Violence: From Research to Practice.* Mahwah, NJ: Lawrence Erlbaum.

Partnership for Family Involvement in Education. (n.d.). *Steps you can take to improve your children's education.* Retrieved on January 4, 2011, from http://www2 .ed.gov/pubs/PFIE/families.html

Pearson, P., Barr, R., Mosenthal, P., & Kamil, M. (Eds.). (2000). *Handbook of reading research* (Vol. 3). Mahwah, NJ: Lawrence Erlbaum Associates.

Pearson Education. (2009). *SuccessMaker.* Retrieved from http://www.pearsonschool .com/index.cfm?locator=PSZk99

Penuel, W., Fishman, B., Yamaguchi, R., & Gallagher, L. (2007). What makes professional development effective? Strategies that foster curriculum implementation. *American Educational Research Journal, 44*(4), 921–958.

Perie, M., Griggs, W.S., Donahue, P.L. (2005). *The nation's report card: Reading 2005* (NCES 2006-451). Retrieved January 13, 2011, from http://nces.ed.gov/pubsearch/pubsinfo.asp?pubid=2006451

Peter Kirk Elementary. (2010). *Peter Kirk's mission and vision statement.* Retrieved January 17, 2011, from http://www.lwsd.org/school/kirk/About-Us/Pages/Mission-and-vision-statement.aspx

Peterson, R.L., & Schoonover, B. (2008, June). *Fact sheet #3: Zero tolerance policies in schools.* Retrieved September 24, 2010, from http://www.preventschoolviolence.org/resources_assets/CPSV-Fact-Sheet-3-Zero-Tolerance.pdf

Peterson, R.L., & Skiba, R. (2001). Creating school climates that prevent school violence. *Social Studies, 92*(4), 167–175.

Piasta, S., Connor, C., Fishman, B., & Morrison, F. (2009). Teachers' knowledge of literacy concepts, classroom practices, and student reading growth. *Scientific Studies of Reading, 13*(3), 224–248.

Plessy v. Ferguson, 163 U.S. 537 (1896).

Popham, W.J. (2007). *Classroom assessment: What teachers need to know* (5th ed.). Boston: Pearson Education.

Prince, S.B., & Taylor, R.G. (1995). Should the correlates of effective schools be used as prescription for improving achievement? *Educational Research Quarterly, 18*(4), 19–26.

Raffaele, L., & Knoff, H. (1999). Improving home-school collaboration with disadvantaged families: Organizational principles, perspectives, and approaches. *The School Psychology Review, 28*(3), 448–466.

Rangel, E.S. (2007). Time to learn. *American Educational Research Association Research Points, 5*(2), 1–4.

Ratcliffe, M.J.A. (2006). *A study of the relationship between the correlates of effective schools and aggregate adequate yearly progress.* Retrieved February 23, 2011, from gradworks.umi.com/32/56/3256628.html

Ravitch, D. (2000). *Left back: A century of failed school reforms.* New York: Simon and Shuster.

Ray, J. (2005). Family-friendly teachers: Tips for working with diverse families. *Kappa Delta Pi Record, 41*(2), 72–76.

Reading First Notebook. (2005, Spring). *What is instructional leadership, and why is it so important?* Retrieved January 11, 2011, from http://www.sedl.org/pubs/reading100/RF-NB-2005-Spring.pdf

Redbeck Black, A., Doolittle, F., Zhu, P., Unterman, R., & Baldwin Grossman, G. (2008). *The evaluation of enhanced academic instruction in after-school programs: Findings after the first year implementation.* Retrieved January 15, 2011, from http://www.mdrc.org/publications/480/overview.html

Rice, J. (2003). *Teacher quality: Understanding the effectiveness of teacher attributes.* Washington, DC: Economic Policy Institute.

Riley, R.W. (1994, September). *Strong families, strong schools* [Remarks prepared for speech to National Press Club, Washington, D.C.]. Retrieved January 17, 2011, from http://www2.ed.gov/Speeches/09-1994/strong.html

Robbins, P., & Alvy, H. (2004). *The new principal's fieldbook strategies for success.* Alexandria, VA: Association for Supervision and Curriculum Development.

Romi, S., & Leyser, Y. (2006). Exploring inclusion preservice training needs: A study of variables associated with attitudes and self-efficacy beliefs. *European Journal of Special Needs Education, 21*(1), 85–105. Retrieved June 3, 2009, from E-Journals database.

Rubin, B. (2006). Tracking and detracking: Debates, evidence, and best practices for a heterogeneous world. *Theory Into Practice, 45*(1), 4–14. Retrieved March 4, 2007, from the Academic Search Premier database.

Rutter, M. (1983). School effect on pupil progress: Research findings and policy implications. In L. Shulman & G. Sykes (Eds.), *Handbook of teaching and policy* (pp. 3–41). New York: Longman.

Rutter, M., Maughan, B., Ouston, J., & Smith, A. (1979). *Fifteen thousand hours: Secondary schools and their effects on children.* Cambridge, MA: Harvard University Press.

Safe Schools Assessment and Resource Bank. (n.d.). *Introduction to the Safe Schools Assessment and Resource Bank.* Retrieved January 17, 2011, from http://www.ssarb .com/introduction.aspx#benefits

Safer, N., & Fleischman, S. (2005). Research matters: How student progress monitoring improves instruction. *Educational Leadership, 62*(5), 81–83.

Sass, E. (2005). *American educational history: A hypertext timeline.* Retrieved January 17, 2011, from http://www.cloudnet.com/~edrbsass/educationhistorytimeline.html

Scheerens, J., & Bosker, R.J. (1997). *The foundation of educational effectiveness.* Oxford, United Kingdom: Elsevier Science.

Schmidt, R.J., Rozendal, M.S., & Greenman, G.G. (2002). Reading instruction in the inclusion classroom: Research-based practices. *Remedial and Special Education, 23*(3), 130. Retrieved March 4, 2007, from ERIC database.

School improvement in Maryland. (2009). Retrieved from http://mdk12.org

Services, S.W. (n.d.). *Safe schools assessment and resource bank (SSARB).* Retrieved September 24, 2010, from http://store.cambiumlearning.com/ProgramPage.aspx? parentId=019005320&functionID=009000008&pID=&site=sw

Shedlin, A. (2004). Is your school father-friendly? *Principal, 83*(3), 22–25.

Soodak, L.C., Podell, D.M., & Lehman, L.R. (1998) Teacher, student and school attributes as predictors of teachers' responses to inclusion, *Journal of Special Education, 31*(4), 480–497.

Sopris West Educational Services. (n.d.). *Safe schools assessment and resource bank.* Retrieved September 14, 2010, from http://www.ssarb.com/SSISHome.aspx

Stringfield, S. (2004). *Effective schools implementation in the 21st century: Resource readings* (4th ed.). Louisville, KY: University of Louisville.

Taylor, B. (2009). *Classroom management impacts student achievement: Tips to thrive and survive.* Retrieved January 17, 2011, from http://www.eric.ed.gov/PDFS/ ED506815.pdf

Teddlie, C., & Stringfield, S. (1993). *Schools make a difference: Lessons learned from a 10-year study of school effects.* New York: Teachers College Press.

Tichenor, M.S. (1998). Teacher education and parent involvement: Reflections from pre-service teachers. *Journal of Instructional Psychology, 24,* 233–239.

Tieso, C. (2003). Ability grouping is not just tracking anymore. *Roeper Review, 26*(1), 29–36.

Tsay, M., & Brady, M. (2010). A case study of cooperative learning and communication pedagogy: Does working in teams make a difference? *Journal of the Scholarship of Teaching and Learning, 10*(2), 78–89.

Tschannen-Moran, M., & Woolfolk-Hoy, A. (2001). Teacher efficacy: Capturing an elusive construct. *Teaching and Teacher Education, 17*(6), 783–805.

Uchida, C.D., Maguire, E.R., Solomon, S.E., & Gantley, M. (2004, December). *Safe kids, safe schools: Evaluating the use of iris recognition technology in New Egypt, NJ.* Retrieved September 24, 2010, from http://www.ncjrs.gov/pdffiles1/nij/grants/ 208127.pdf

University of Oregon, Center on Teaching and Learning. (n.d.). *DIBELS Data System.* Retrieved from https://dibels.uoregon.edu

U.S. Census Bureau. (2004). *Current population survey (CPS): Definitions and explanations.* Retrieved January 17, 2011, from http://www.census.gov/population/www/cps/cpsdef.html

U.S. Department of Education. (n.d.-a). *Improving basic programs operated by local education agencies (Title I, part A).* Retrieved September 3, 2005, from http://www.ed.gov/programs/titleiparta/index.html

U.S. Department of Education. (n.d.-b). *Safe Schools/Healthy Students (SS/HS) grant application kit.* Retrieved February 22, 2011, from http://www.sshs.samhsa.gov/apply/kit.aspx

U.S. Department of Education (n.d.-c). *School connectedness and meaningful student participation.* Retrieved January 4, 2011, from http://www2.ed.gov/admins/lead/safety/training/connect/school_pg3.html

U.S. Department of Education. (2002). *No Child Left Behind: A desktop reference.* Retrieved January 26, 2006, from http://www.ed.gov/admins/lead/account/nclbreference/page_pg3.html

U.S. Department of Education. (2003). *When schools stay open late: The national evaluation of the 21st-century learning centers program, first year findings.* Washington, DC: Author.

U.S. Department of Education. (2004). *No child left behind: A toolkit for teachers.* Washington, DC: Author.

U.S. Department of Education. (2008). *Peer review guidance for the NCLB differentiated accountability pilot applications.* Retrieved March 16, 2011, from http://www2.ed.gov/policy/elsec/guid/daguidance.doc

U.S. Department of Education. (2009a). *The American recovery and reinvestment act of 2009: Saving and creating jobs and reforming education.* Retrieved July 28, 2010, from http://www2.ed.gov/policy/gen/leg/recovery/implementation.html

U.S. Department of Education. (2009b). *Secretary Arne Duncan speaks at the 91st annual meeting of the American council on education.* Retrieved July 28, 2010, from http://www.ed.gov/news/speeches/secretary-arne-duncan-speaks-91st-annual-meeting-american-council-education

U.S. Department of Education. (2010a). *A blueprint for reform: The reauthorization of the elementary and secondary education act.* Retrieved July 28, 2010, from http://www2.ed.gov/policy/elsec/leg/blueprint/blueprint.pdf

U.S. Department of Education. (2010b). *Education secretary Duncan issues statement on the nation's report card in reading for 4th, 8th graders.* Retrieved July 28, 2010, from http://www2.ed.gov/news/pressreleases/2010/03/03242010.html

U.S. Department of Education. (2010c). *Nine states and the District of Columbia win second round race to the top grants.* Retrieved January 1, 2011, from http://www2.ed.gov/news/pressreleases/nine-states-and-district-columbia-win-second-race-top-grants

Van de Grift, W., & Houtveen, A.A.M. (1999). Educational leadership and pupil achievement in primary education. *School Effectiveness and School Improvement, 10,* 373–389.

van der Graaf, V.K. (2008). *A five year comparison between an extended year school and a conventional year school: Effects on academic achievement.* Unpublished doctoral dissertation, Lindenwood University.

Viadero, D. (2008). Research yields clues on the effects of extra time for learning. *Education Week, 28*(5), 16–17.

Villanova, R., Gauthier, W., Proctor, P., & Shoemaker, J. (1981). *Connecticut School Effectiveness Questionnaire.* Hartford, CT: Bureau of School Improvement.

Waters, T., Marzano, R.J., & McNulty, B. (2003). *What 30 years of research tells us about the effect of leadership on student achievement: A working paper.* Retrieved January 17, 2011, from http://www.sai-iowa.org/storage/BalancedLeadership.pdf

Weber, G. (1971). *Inner-city children can be taught to read: Four successful schools.* Washington, DC: Council for Basic Education.

Weiss, I.R., Pasley, J.D., Smith, P.S., Banilower, E.R., & Heck, D.J. (2003). *Looking inside the classroom: A study of K-12 mathematics and science education in the United States.* Chapel Hill, NC: Horizon Research.

WestED Policy Brief. (2001). *Time and learning. Making time count.* Retrieved January 17, 2011, from http://www.wested.org/cs/we/view/rs/535

White, L. (1998). National PTA standards for parent/family involvement programs. *High School Magazine, 5,* 8–12.

White House Blog. (2009). *Taking on education.* Retrieved July 28, 2010, from http://www.whitehouse.gov/blog/2009/03/10/taking-education

Winn, D.D., Hobbs, D.E., & Johnson, F.F. (1998). Reweaving the tapestry of teacher education. *The Teacher Educator, 33*(4), 260–273.

Winn, P., Erwin, S., Gentry, J., & Cauble, M. (2009, April). *Rural principal skills and student achievement.* Paper presented at the meeting of Learning and Teaching in Educational Leadership SIG AERA, San Diego, CA.

Wong, H.K., & Wong, R.T. (2009). *The first days of school: How to be an effective teacher.* Mountain View, CA: Harry K. Wong.

Yara, P.O. (2009). Relationship between teachers' attitude and students' academic achievement in mathematics in some selected senior secondary schools in southwestern Nigeria. *European Journal of Social Sciences, 11*(3), 364.

Zellman, G.I., & Waterman, J.M. (1998). Understanding the impact of parent school involvement on children's educational outcomes. *Journal of Educational Research, 91*(6), 370–380.

Zmuda, A., Kuklis, R., & Kline, E. (2004). *Transforming schools: Creating a culture of continuous improvement.* Alexandria, VA: Association for Supervision and Curriculum Development.

Index

Page numbers followed by *t* and *f* indicate tables and figures, respectively.